I Planted the Seed
(and Woody Squashed it)

Unless otherwise indicated, all Scripture is taken from the HOLY
BIBLE, NEW INTERNATIONAL VERSION Copyright © 1973, 1978,
1984 International Bible Society.
Used by permission of Zondervan Bible Publishers.

Library of Congress Cataloging-in-Publishing Data

Phillips, Barry D.

I Planted the Seed (and Woody Squashed it)

By Barry Phillips [2nd edition], 2012

Includes bibliographical references

ISBN 978-0-615-52594-5

Topics: Religion, Christian, Missions BV2000-3705

Anecdotes and characters included in this volume are based on actual
events or people. Some may be composites of actual events and
people. Names and details have been changed to protect identities.

Cover photo by Josh Boren

Cover Art by Jesse Dean Rivero Phillips

Published by globalwarmth publishing
1356 Wendell Lane, Grovetown, GA 30813
e-mail: globalwarmth@gmail.com
Author's website: barrydeanphillips.com

Foreword

The scene still remains clearly etched in my mind . . . and upon my heart. It was my first short-term mission trip to the Philippines. I was joined on this mission with over thirty people from our church who had left behind the comforts of home to take the Gospel to people we had never met. We were excited, nervous, but also expectant that God would use our efforts to lead many to a new relationship with Jesus Christ.

Standing in the rocky parking area of Malupa Baptist Church (which was utilized by jeepneys and tricycles rather than trucks and cars), I heard the not so melodious sound of a band as it traveled closer and closer to the church. As the band came into sight, I was just a little shocked but also much amused to find that the band consisted of a long line of elementary-aged school kids! These kids were as enthusiastic as any college marching band during halftime of a Saturday football game. With smiles from ear to ear, they played their instruments with gusto. And leading the parade, as official band leader at the head of the line, was our missionary host, Barry Phillips. In all my time building a friendship with him and serving alongside of him in our church back home, I had never ever seen him more in his element than at that moment.

Perhaps the reason that this scene is so easily remembered is because it is the perfect reminder that reaching people requires our surrender. We will never reach them from the sidelines. We must get into the game . . . their game . . . on their turf . . . in their part of the world. It is only then that our lives can truly make a difference in their lives.

Jesus' ministry was incarnational in nature in that He left the perfection of Heaven to live His earthly life within the context of a fallen world. During His ministry captured so well in the Gospels, He lived a perfect and sinless life in an imperfect and fallen world. He came to us and met us at our greatest point of need because He loved us enough to give Himself in our place. Today, He calls His followers to do much the same. Not as saviors to the world but in ultimate service to the only Savior of the world. We heed His call when we take His message of the Gospel to those who are desperately in need of Him. We can reach them no other way but by going to them.

As I read *"I Planted the Seed"*, my memories of three trips to the Philippines came flooding back. Barry has a way of relating life from "the ends of the earth" in a clear, accurate, and compelling way. Reading of his experiences will create in you a desire to involve yourself in missions so that your life can be used by God to change the life of another. His experience and insight are invaluable in preparing others to travel cross-culturally for the purpose of missions. He holds nothing back as he delves into the challenges of short-term missions which often are learned the hard way through poor planning and poor preparation. Whether you travel to this beautiful country or whether the Lord leads you to take His message to another region of the world, you will be much better prepared by reading and applying the principles found here.

Little did I know that when Barry, Lilia, Jesse, and Dylan Phillips breezed into our church one hot summer day in July that God would see fit to begin a work though our church family that would extend onward for years. This work would enable us to play a part in fulfilling the Great Commission and in going with the Gospel to a land far away. This work would be accomplished by the Lord through us but would begin when He sent the Phillips' to us.

I treasure my friendship with Barry and his wonderful family. I have witnessed firsthand the difference that a yielded life can make when one is willing to follow God's lead and trust Him with the results. I know you will be challenged, encouraged, and equipped by this great book and my hope is that you will determine to allow the Lord to use your life as a platform for His glory, even if that means taking His message further than you ever dreamed!

Brooks Cail
Senior Pastor
First Baptist Church of the Islands
Savannah, Georgia

I0163347

Acknowledgments

Jesse and Dylan, my sons, grew up as missionary kids (MK's) in the Philippines and are an inspiration to me. MK's, as a lot, are awesome! They return infrequently to their "home" country and have only a tenuous link to their parent's culture. MK's spend their childhoods and formative years as an ethnic minority, yet assimilate themselves into the culture where they live. They learn and speak the local language, appreciate the native food, and gain perspectives that are broader than those of their peers "back home."

For many MK's, the first extended stay in their ancestral home nation is when they leave behind the only culture they know and people that they truly love to "return home" to college life. But, if nothing else, MK's are adaptable. While they may be ignorant about American pop culture or popular television personalities, they adjust quickly to their environment. Jesse has already *transformed* back into an American, but I know that he doesn't take simple things for granted such as: air conditioning, public libraries, high speed internet, fast food restaurants or uninterrupted electricity.

We were delighted when Jesse graduated from Liberty University three months ago, and excited to see what the Lord will do though him as session musician in Nashville. We miss him terribly, and I know that he senses the many thousands of miles between us. Our next reunion will be sweet. Dylan, my youngest child, will soon be departing to the US to attend college. I've been his teacher since kindergarten and we've spent an enormous amount of time together. I'm sure we'll cope as he transitions to life in the US, but our hearts will break when he gets on the plane to leave.

My sons have endured years without television, internet, or hot water. They hide their frustration when the electricity dies, and they get as excited as I do with each approaching typhoon. They are mature beyond their years precisely because of hardship they've endured. They can live without the *things* their friends enjoy back in "the world." I'm blessed that the Lord has allowed me to father such remarkable young men and am forever grateful for the love that they show to their mother and to me.

Contents

Attachments

End Notes

Introduction

The number of short-term North American missionaries has swollen from a few hundred people per year in the mid-1960s to upward of a million people per year. Some estimates are much higher, suggesting that close to four million people will participate in short-term missions this year (2011.) The cost of these short term trips now surpasses the total financial support provided to full time missionaries. Mobilizing four million people is a colossal undertaking; that's more than four times the number of foreign troops deployed to Iraq in support of Operation Desert Storm!

At this moment enormous logistical effort begins within the walls of tens of thousands of churches and mission agencies in preparation for short-term mission trips. Pastors, church administrators, and a variety of volunteers tackle the necessary arrangements. They acquire tickets for travel, obtain insurance, book accommodations, plan meals, review security plans, assist with applications for passports and visas, investigate customs requirements, and assess authorization requirements to accompany minors. These leaders are examining country-unique requirements while attempting to prepare for "just in case" or "what if" plans. The annual effort to mobilize Christian missionaries to every region of the planet is truly monumental, presenting an overwhelming task beyond the realm of their knowledge and capabilities.

I've led several short-term mission teams and was able to locate a variety of resources to help spiritually prepare a team. In preparation for a trip, you'll discover scores of devotional books specifically designed to instill a missionary heart. This isn't one of them. Spiritual preparation is vital and necessary, but *I Planted the Seed (and Woody Squashed it)* was written to prepare you and your team for your mission in a different way. It will prepare you for the practical aspects of missions as well as the spiritual aspects.

Your team's travels will expose you to many places and oftentimes, challenging surroundings that will be unlike anything you've experienced before. Within these pages, I'll address issues that are as small as the tiniest insects or exotic microbes, to poisonous plant wounds that can be incapacitating. Knowledge of minute monetary details will be shared, including currency regulations which may prevent a team member from discovering that travelers' checks are worthless in some countries.

In short, *I Planted the Seed (and Woody Squashed it)* compels you to examine safety, security and health issues. It illuminates many stark cultural differences that you'll experience. It will strive to open your eyes to consider how you'll respond to beggars, lepers, drunks or armed insurgents. It examines team member suitability, and explains why some people should not participate. You'll be better prepared to deal with determining which items should be carried with you versus those purchased from a local source while on mission.

As a full time missionary in the Philippines I've hosted teams from a variety of locations and have witnessed: illicit romances, serious illness, emotional breakdowns, allergic reactions, team discord, individual rebellion, collective fear, and remarkable compassion. Some teams truly acted as a team, showing concern for one another and sacrificing personal comfort to accommodate a team member. Other 'teams' have caused us embarrassment with ugly verbal exchanges in front of our Filipino brothers and sisters. We once hosted two young women from the same church who refused even to speak to one another during their stay. Putting Christ on display requires more than words. You, as team members, must be willing to submit to your team leader's guidance. And you, as team leaders, need to be able to demonstrate the attributes of Christ in the midst of chaos and be willing to challenge behavior or attitudes that might damage the cause of Christ.

Some people question the cost effectiveness of short term missions, arguing that it costs just as much to send a handful of semi-trained missionaries for two weeks into another culture as to support a full-time missionary family there for a year. Others will argue that short-term missions create a sense of dependence, stifling the development of self-supporting, self-replicating indigenous churches. And they would be correct in this belief; indigenous churches often postpone activities or projects until the return of their wealthy missionary friends.

Some 'career' missionaries don't welcome short term visitors because they don't want their ministry damaged by *"short-term workers who wear clothes that local people see as indecent, give gifts that are extravagant in a Third World country and make promises they can't keep ..."* [i] Miriam Adeney, says, *"What nurses and doctors are taught is appropriate for missionaries too: 'First, do no harm.' 'To say that "something is better than nothing," is no justification for poor missions work. Some missions work--even though it stimulates us-can be worse than nothing."* [1]

Count me, though, as a believer in short term missions. But I'm even more fervent in my belief that short term missions must be carefully aligned with the plans and long-term strategy of the ministry being served. If properly planned and managed, short term missions

---

[1] Published in the spring 1998 issue of Enrichment Journal. Used with permission.

will benefit the sending church, the missionaries, and the overseas ministry. These trips are transformational in the lives of many missionaries who return home with new vitality and a sense of purpose in Christ. Poverty becomes personal to them, and now has a name and a face. Many, for the first time, become aware of their abundance (excess) and are transformed into givers. I pray that if you are planning or participating, you may be transformed more into the likeness of Christ as a result of participating in short term missions.

Jesus told his disciples to, "Ask the Lord of the harvest, therefore, to send workers into his harvest field. " (Matthew 9:38) Could the Lord send them without being asked to do so? After all, they are *His* harvest fields. The Lord knows that we can't continuously pray, "Lord, please send *someone else* to help in your harvest" without experiencing an awakening. God doesn't want you to pray for someone else to go, he wants *you* to go. I pray that your short term missionary experience will lead to a lifetime commitment to missions.

I also pray that *I Planted the Seed (and Woody Squashed it)* will make you more productive as you serve Christ in another culture. I'm grateful for your willingness to serve, and pray to our Heavenly Father that your efforts will bear fruit in another culture. Stay healthy and safe, but more importantly, remain faithful to the Lamb of God in whom salvation is found. Allow the pages of this book to transform

your travels into a destination that will touch and changes lives,

including yours.

Whatever!

"Whatever." It's a word that implies a non-caring attitude, perhaps the response a rebellious teenager tosses out to a strict parent. I'm always concerned when someone signs up for 'whatever' as we plan our mission trips. First, it suggests that they haven't discovered how God has gifted them. It's like signing up for an orchestra and when asked what instrument they play the reply is 'whatever'. It's unlikely that they excel playing every instrument. They may, in fact, play most instruments quite poorly. So why wouldn't they sign up for clarinet if they shine at it, or tuba if it's truly what they play best. Why should God accept 'whatever'?

Please don't misunderstand what I'm saying. It's important for us to step out of our comfort zone from time-to-time. Deuteronomy 31:8 says: *"The Lord himself goes before you and will be with you; he will never leave you nor forsake you. Do not be afraid. Do not be discouraged."* God uses new circumstances to stretch and grow us.

That's why you shouldn't sign up for a construction team, then complain that the heat is oppressive, or that you never got to see anything except the construction site. *You signed up to be on the construction team*! So before you sign up for a mission trip, please evaluate your talents. Consider what you enjoy or dislike doing, and pray about your participation. And when you commit yourself, don't sign up for 'whatever'.

Even if you're not sure how you'll be used, if the Lord is leading you to go, obey the prompting of the Holy Spirit. You need to go. In fact, you *must* go. If the creator of the universe calls you to participate, what suitable excuse can you offer for remaining home? A young man from our church in the U.S. signed up to participate on three separate mission trips. He attended every team meeting, prayed and shared his testimony with the team. He sent out letters to raise support for his trip(s), however, when he received only a fraction of the support money needed, he backed out each time with the opening of each envelope. He told me that he felt "called" to participate, so I asked him the obvious question, *"Then why aren't you coming along?"* His answer still breaks my heart. He replied, "The *airfare alone would eat up most of my savings.*"

His answer indicates, first of all, that his beliefs were based on his ownership of the money in his bank. But the truth is that his money and possessions belonged to God – as stewards we are only managers and caretakers. Psalm 24:1 states it clearly: *"The earth is the Lord's, and everything in it, the world, and all who live in it."* So, in essence, he was unwilling to use the Lord's money to do what the Lord called him to do. But just as perplexing was his reliance on others as a condition to follow God. He was willing to use their money, but not his own. And if they failed to provide 'adequate' assistance he'd disobey God. When God calls you to go, you have two options: go or disobey.

It's been my experience that commitment also precedes provision, and clarity is provided in the midst of obedience. God has answered my needs only after I step out in faith, not beforehand. God tests our hearts, and the most frequent test seems to involve money. How can we stand before the judgment throne of Christ and explain, *"They just never sent me enough money to cover the trip."* Personally, I'd sell my car, take on a part-time job, or charge the airfare to my credit card. Jesus makes it clear that we can't serve both God and money; I choose God. So should you.

You'll discover that many of the most powerful moments experienced on mission trips are not moments that were planned. If you pay attention, you'll notice that God planned some *divine appointments* for you. The senior pastor of our church in Savannah, Georgia shared such an incident. As he was coming down from the mountains he saw the Philippine Sea in the distance and asked his driver to stop so that he could take a picture. Moments later two shirtless men carrying machetes came crashing out of the bushes. It was a divine appointment, and our pastor recognized it as such. He seized the opportunity to tell them about Jesus, and both men prayed with him to receive Jesus as their Lord and Savior.

Our vehicle ran out of gas and the entire family in the nearest home became believers as a result of us retreating to their tiny grass hut for assistance. We had a flat tire and the man who came to assist us became a brother in Christ. I now get excited when something unplanned happens. God uses his divine intervention during such moments, but missionaries need to be alert to them.

Even though most of the 'divine appointments' are unplanned, planning remains an essential element for successful short term mission trips. Find out from your host what is needed or what's been most effective in the past.

Too many churches send teams that conduct ministries that don't add value to the host ministry. If you told me that you were considering bringing a team here to do sports ministry, I'd advise against it for reasons illustrated here. Nearly a decade ago Hands of Hope International assisted in starting a "Christian" basketball league here. The teams prayed together before every game, but within minutes of the opening tipoff, unsportsmanlike behavior became obviously prevalent. Someone threw an intentional elbow to an opponent's mouth, followed by a foul-mouthed retaliation with pushing and shoving. Moments later a fistfight broke out. Christ received no glory from our "Christian" basketball league. In the heat of competition, with bodies banging together beneath the hoop, the potential for damage to the mission and the local ministry increased exponentially.

If you're a boxing coach, or a martial arts enthusiast, use those talents to minister to people at home. Although sports ministries can be successful, creating strong bonds of trust and producing true camaraderie, there isn't enough time on a two week trip to properly train and condition participants. Injuries often take over. The potential downside is greater than the benefit to our ministry if we employ the protective head gear and boxing gloves you brought along. I might accidently hurt someone or, more likely, get my aging ribs broken if I square off with one of my junior pastors for a few rounds. Contact sports, in my assessment, are risky short-term ministry tools. Don't be forever immortalized by the words, "*He started it!*"

Therefore, since we are surrounded by such a great cloud of witnesses, let us throw off everything that hinders and the sin that so easily entangles, and let us run with perseverance the race marked out for us. - Hebrews 12:1

Chapter One Discussion Questions

1. Do you feel 'called' to go?

2. How will you fund the trip?

3. Are you signed up for something more specific than 'whatever'?

4. How closely does your planned participation on this mission trip align with your spiritual gifts?

5. Is there a detailed schedule of activities in which you'll participate?

6. Is there room in your schedule for divine appointments?

7. Damage assessment: do any of your planned ministry activities have the potential to cause discord? (Jealousy, envy, resentment, anger or physical injury?)

Who's in charge?

This chapter is addressed primarily to team leaders, but also explains why team members need to submit to their team leader's guidance.

Offensive behavior, if not challenged by your team leader, will frustrate your team, upset your host missionary, and diminish your effectiveness. There are clearly times that you, as team leader, must take charge and assert yourself as the leader of your team. Your host missionary should never have to discipline or counsel your team members. Team leaders may be forced to challenge the following inappropriate behaviors:

- Poor attitudes - pouting, whining, arguing, temper tantrums, incessant complaints;

- Inappropriate attire- tight, too much exposed skin, T-shirts with offensive graphics or words;

- Unkind words - insensitive, sarcastic, vulgar, or hurtful;

- Poor money management - borrowing from team members (or from your host);

- Lack of participation - opting to remain sequestered in their room or in the travel vehicle to avoid assisting with team duties;

- Team covenant violations - smoking, alcohol possession etc.

- Flirtation among team members or those who are to be ministered to.

- Rampant gossip about fellow team members.

If leaders fail to challenge unacceptable behavior, they discover that others on the team may step in and try to deal with it. The results of this behavior are evident in bickering, sure signs of weak leadership. If a designated team leader simply can't discipline others, an optional respected team member should be appointed to provide counsel to other team members. Team members should be informed regarding who is responsible for correcting improper behavior during the trip.

It's possible that a team member may become so uncooperative or break enough team rules that they need to be sent home early. I've had one such case. At the time there was no policy that defined the ifs and hows to send a rule-breaker home. Who, if anyone, will accompany the scoundrel through the rough and mountainous roads back to an airport? Who will be responsible for paying for the miscreant's meals or hotel once he leaves the team?

How will costs associated with flight changes be handled? What if the degenerate is a minor? How can we ensure the reprobate's safety? We endured an extra week of rebellion and a putrid attitude from an imposter 'missionary' because we didn't have any defined procedure in place to send him home. The team, and the mission, suffered as a result. Before you travel you'll need to define and share the process you'll use to send misfits home early.

The harshness of those statements is based on reality. However, believers must be guided by Christ-like behavior, even in discipling rule-breakers. . And when a team member (a fellow brother or sister in Christ) does something wrong, even something considered as *unpardonable,* the goal is not to send them home in disgrace. Restoration and grace is preferred, and leaders may be required to demonstrate that they possess the fruits of the spirit. After all, it's the offender, not the righteous to whom God extends grace. Christian leadership must be, first of all, patient. And as a team leader, your patience *will* be tested. How will you react when:

- Its 5:30 AM, thirty minutes past your scheduled departure to the airport, and five of your team members haven't arrived?

- A team member leaves the airport concourse to go to McDonald's *after* the first class passengers have already boarded your international flight?

- A team member becomes disrespectful with the ticket counter agent over seating assignments?

- A team member carries along three extra oversized, *personal* bags?

- You're at the airport and a team member can't find his passport?

- Three team members fail to return from lunch to the team bus in a mall parking lot, and remain missing for over 90 minutes?

- Two team members decide to leave the hotel after midnight in Manila to "see the sights?"

All of these incidents have occurred on actual trips. And note: These are only travel-related issues. A team leader's patience *will* be tested, and you need to prepare your response in advance. Some things demand a response (such as ugly behavior at the ticket counter) while other issues, such as extra bags, won't change as a result of your reaction.

The answers are clear. Choose your battles – some are not worth fighting, but others shouldn't be avoided. Thomas Jefferson said, *"In matters of style, swim with the current; in matters of principle, stand like a rock."* Review the rules with the entire team so that nobody has any question about the suitability of wearing a 'speedo' or a 'thong' bikini on your sightseeing day.

It's embarrassing to ask someone to change their clothes because what they are wearing is deemed to be 'inappropriate' attire, so please don't put your team leader in such a position. What passes as completely acceptable attire in your hometown may be considered provocative in another culture. This advice will work in virtually any culture: when you participate in missions, dress like you're a school teacher. It's that simple. Some cultures are *very* conservative regarding dress, and are shocked or offended when you show too much bare leg, your belly button, or, *God forbid*, cleavage. The Philippines is not one of those places, but we've hosted several visitors who have crossed the line of propriety. Nothing was ever said by the team leader, but trust me, we heard plenty of commentary from the locals.

It's easy to differentiate between teams that arrive prepared and those that come as a cluster of individuals. It requires time to build a team. They pray together, share their testimonies, plan their trip together, and spend time getting to know one another before they get on the airplane. They know why they are going, what they hope to accomplish, who they will be serving, and they possess a basic understanding of the culture. I experienced one 'team' that arrived in the Philippines and I knew all of their names before they did. Take time to build a team before you travel. Eat together frequently. Meet your team member's families. Share your concerns with them. It will make life much easier when you're sharing cramped communal living space.

God is in charge! That's the answer to the question in the title of this chapter. And as team leader, insure that your plans are God-centered, not team-centered. Seek the Lord's desire for your team, not your team's desire for the trip. Don't take twenty people on a mission that requires ten – establish your optimal team size and be willing to set limits. If there are far more who want to go than are needed, plan another trip. But in all your plans, please recognize that we are merely clay in His hands, and that the fruit of our efforts belong to Him, not us.

Our mission team gave a report to the church one Sunday morning after a 'successful' trip to the Philippines. A visitor at church listened to the testimony of three missionaries and came to the conclusion that the church was 'patting itself on the back' for accomplishments during the mission trip. She filled out a visitor's card that expressed dismay regarding our testimonies; she felt that we boasted about what "*we*" did instead of what *God* did through us. I disagree with her assessment of our team's testimony, but it's a sobering thought to consider that we try to take credit for what only God can do. Mission teams are comprised of His hands and feet, and need to understand that fact as we plan, organize and conduct our mission trips.

Jesus tells us to feed the hungry, yet he never suggests that the result of our obedience will end world hunger. In fact, our obsession with results can cause us to miss the point. We lift the burden of the poor to serve Christ. Matthew 26:11 says, "*The poor you will always have with you, but you will not always have me.*" We will not end poverty through our effort, but we are able to put Christ on display as we serve the poor. And whatever we do to aid the sick, homeless, poor, or hungry we do for Christ. (Matthew 25:40)

You don't need to be a strong personality to lead a team of missionaries. But you must be strong in your faith and willing to be firm on matters of principle. Enforce the team covenant, encourage team unity, and strengthen every ministry you visit.

You turn things upside down, as if the potter were thought to be like the clay! Shall what is formed say to him who formed it, "He did not make me"? Can the pot say of the potter, "He knows nothing"? - Isaiah 29:16

Chapter Two Discussion Questions

1. Who is your team leader?

2. Have you honestly submitted to the authority of your team leader?

3. Have you signed a team covenant that prescribes behavior while on the mission trip?

4. Are you concerned with anything in the team covenant? If so, have you discussed your concern or asked for prayer?

5. Is your attitude one of cooperation?

6. Have you been meeting regularly with other team members?

7. Are you prepared to experience inconvenience without complaining?

8. What does your team plan to accomplish during the trip?

9. Have adequate background checks been performed on each of the team members?

3 Too proud to ask

A sizeable mission team from a Methodist church in Athens, Georgia visited our remote region of the Aurora Province of the Philippines to construct a parsonage, work on a college building, and meet medical needs. Always curious about missions, I inquired about their fundraising tasks and discovered that they enjoyed a unique blessing. They're located a few blocks from the University of Georgia football stadium and utilized their parking lot to rent their parking lot to football fans. They offer season passes, stipulating that their parking slot would be sold for the day if not occupied thirty minutes before game time. They used the proceeds from their parking lot to support their summer mission trips.

This parking lot mission was organized, financially accountable to the church, and properly staffed by born-again Christian church members. Although their missionaries are fully supported, the church still required effort to manage the parking lot. Each parking slot must be sold, parking passes issued, records kept, and people have to manage the parking lot on game day. Churches hold a variety of fund raising events to help missionaries: car washes, church yard sales, raffles, bake sales, and contests. In short, the list of fundraising

activities is deep and diverse. Think about the magnitude of the effort

to raise roughly **eight billion dollars** (four million North American

missionaries who require an average of around $2000 per traveler.)

That's an enormous amount of commerce! Can we sell enough

cookies or wash enough cars to raise eight *billion* dollars? I don't

think so.

Let's face reality. Most fund raising efforts fall short, and mission

teams need to ask for help. They compose heartfelt support letters

inviting friends, family, neighbors, co-workers, classmates, (even their

doctors, dentists and mail carriers), to participate in their trip

financially and through prayer. Teams pray over these letters then

mail them out and wait for people to respond. It's interesting to see

the result; some will receive many times the amount needed within

two weeks. Others, when the deadline arrives, will have received a

total of less than $100. It's partly a factor of who you know, but your

sincerity and previously *demonstrated* commitment to Christ is also a

factor. Even devout Christians are reluctant to help out if they doubt

the motives. Don't expect any support from people if your faith has

been invisible to them.

It is vital that team members communicate clearly through their

support letters. Some churches supplement the shortfall, providing missionaries with the difference between what a member was able to raise and the actual cost of the trip. Other churches provide no financial assistance. Your supporters need to know the church policy so that they don't assume that you will be assisted by the church if that won't happen. If there are fund-raising efforts aside from sending out support letters, these efforts should also be visible within the church so that everyone is aware of the efforts that are being expended to participate in missions.

And please don't expect the same people to support you every six months! There's a limit to the number of times you can return to the same people for help. Even if they've demonstrated a willingness to participate and have been generous in the past, there's a boundary to their generosity that you don't want to approach. Limit the number of requests to any one person. Our church asks team members not to send support letters to *anyone* in our church family. We didn't want to overwhelm a single church member with twenty (or more) requests for financial assistance. It puts them in an awkward position if they help one or two, but not others.

I've heard people say, "I've never asked anyone for anything" or "I'm not comfortable asking people for help." If your trip was for personal pleasure I'd understand the reluctance. But it's not personal; you're on a mission from God. You've been selected by the creator of the universe to be His servant in another nation. When believers

sense that the Lord is leading you, they feel privileged to participate.

God's people support the Lord's work – they're assisting His effort, not

supporting you. So don't be timid, or too proud, to request

participation from others. There is no need to be apologetic in your

request, i.e., "I realize these are tough economic times and many

people are without jobs, however, … "

Don't limit your support letters to believers – you may be surprised

at the people who will help out. I've received support from non-

Christians who have witnessed the sincerity of my faith. Some may

help out because you're serving impoverished people who need

assistance. Others may support your effort out of friendship; they

have no concern whatsoever about your 'mission' – they just want you

to know that they support *you*. Accept their contributions graciously,

and make a commitment to pray for them. Maybe your mission trip

will open the way for you to share your faith with them.

If you intend to travel with every mission team departing from your

church, consider taking a part-time job to save some extra money. Or

make a proposal to the church staff – you'll help organize, manage,

and lead the trips in exchange for airfare. Properly managed mission

trips require effort, and an overworked youth pastor, worship leader or

administrator may eagerly accept your proposal.

This has been emphasized in the introduction, however, just because the money wasn't provided by someone else doesn't excuse you from participating. Your faithfulness must transcend money. If the Lord has truly called you to participate, go. Don't stand before the Lord on judgment day and try to explain the sad state of your financial situation. He knows. Go!

Whoever serves me must follow me; and where I am, my servant also will be. My Father will honor the one who serves me. - John 12:26

Chapter Three Discussion Questions

1. Do others see a demonstrated commitment to Christ in your life?

2. Describe your service in your home church.

3. Are you afraid to offer others the opportunity to participate financially?

4. If you've been on another mission trip in the past year, are you asking the same people to assist you again?

5. Are you willing to spend your money to pay for the entire trip?

6. What, if anything, can prevent you from being part of this trip?

4 Astonishment

Sweet smoke temporarily blinds us as we drive into a heavy white cloud on our tricycle. Massive piles of burning rice straw, visible from satellites in space, fill the entire region with an unmistakable tang. As soon as we burst out of the smoke canopy the toxic odor of diesel exhaust from a passing truck forces me to cover my nose and mouth with my handkerchief. The aroma of baking bread then wafts into my nostrils and is quickly replaced by the musty smell of water buffalo dung. The smell of burning brake pads now overpowers the dung.

Combinations of odors, experienced only here in the Philippines, team up to create an endless assortment of malodorous stenches and magnificent fragrances. One minute our nasal passages are assaulted by a horrid mix of dead reptile stench mixed with reeking open sewers. Then, as if in apology, we're opt to be treated to the honeysuckle-sweet fragrance of sampaguita's in bloom mixed with the delectable smell of barbeque pork sticks cooking. An instant later the pungent smell of fried dried fish blends with burning rubber from a vulcanizing shop to remind you that you are, indeed, not in Kansas anymore.   As missionaries, our sense of smell is reborn!

I enjoy meeting first time visitors as they arrive at the Manila airport.   Most are in shock.   During the silence and solitude of the flight, perhaps while they slept, flight attendants handed them customs and immigration forms to prepare before disembarking. Humidity, as if it were a living organism, wraps around them tightly as they step from the aircraft. They begin to perspire as they navigate their way through a long plexi-glass maze leading to the immigration counters. They must choose which of the eight lines they belong in. They avoid the "OFW" lane because they don't know what 'OFW' means; the same is true for the "balikbayan" lanes. They choose a line with other Americans they recognize from their flight. More than 200 people are ahead of them in line and, at first they pick up their bags as they inch forward. Soon they simply kick their bags forward, moving only a baby step per minute.

After presenting immigration officials with passports, forms and a quick explanation of their visit, they grab a cart and begin the long search for their belongings. It has taken more than an hour to clear immigration, yet none of the bags from their flights have made it this far. The perspiration has now become a heavy sweat. They move to the baggage carousels to retrieve their luggage and discover that etiquette is different here. A well-dressed woman and two young boys push urgently to the front, as though they needed to grab a passing bag. They grab nothing yet remain in front, next to the revolving baggage carousel. An elderly couple performs the same maneuver, and soon our visitors are standing on their tiptoes, trying to distinguish their large black bag from hundreds of identical bags that return on the turnstile every five minutes. They discover that everyone else also tied a colored ribbon or cloth on the handle for easy identification. If they arrived from the east coast of the United States, their watches have the correct time, only now, it's midnight, not noon.

Uniformed men are everywhere. Some have automatic weapons. Some have shotguns. Some have on white gloves. Sometimes our visitor's hands are shaking due to exhaustion from the trip. For others they are energized by adrenaline from seeing all the guns and uniforms that have them twitching. Most first time visitors have entered into new territory mentally, challenged with thoughts that have never entered their heads before.

Once they clear customs, English signs direct them through the lobby and out of the terminal. If they pay attention, they notice two tunnels across the street and see other passengers pushing their baggage carts into the tunnels. Following the crowd they descend through a steep tunnel, battling against gravity for control of their baggage cart. The noise level amplifies into a confusing cacophony as they reach the street level where we've been waiting for the past two hours to greet them. Our visitors are smiling as they emerge from the tunnel into chaos and disorder, but their eyes belie their dopey grins. They have the bewildered look of refugees escaping a natural disaster or an enemy invasion. The confusion will soon intensify.

Vans and cars are everywhere, each honking its horn as visitors emerge from the tunnel. Police are blowing whistles for no particular reason. One policeman chases a taxicab that is not supposed to be in this area; he fails to catch him, but blows his whistle in short shrill bursts at the driver long after he's departed. Unintelligible announcements blare from loudspeakers every ten seconds, preceded by a tri-tone ring. There are shouts of joy and recognition. Directions are being shouted at drivers, who appear as confused as our visitors. Policemen are shouting at Filipinos who have managed to sneak into the "passengers only" area to await their loved ones. We send a text message to our driver to inform him that we're ready to go.

Our van arrives forty minutes later – the time required to get from the parking area 300 yards away to our pick up location. There's more chaos as we load into our van. We've loaded someone else's bag in the van. Who does this belong to? We return it to the curb and a smiling man thanks us profusely and walks away with the bag. Hopefully it was his. Our driver turns up the radio to 140 decibels. Engelbert Humperdink is singing, "Lonely is a Man Without Love." There's an odd fragrance coming from a banana-looking thing tied to the rearview mirror. It's overpowering and unpleasant – clearly a manufactured smell.

Our driver hasn't moved yet. Another van pulled in front of us and a shirtless driver is loading bags in through the back hatch. He's stopped in the center of the only lane of traffic. Policemen circle around the van and blow their whistles. A policeman with a bullhorn shouts instruction to the driver of the van in front of us, who is still loading bags. He smiles at them and they walk away. Our driver has been holding down his horn, honking one long incessant blast at the illegally parked van in front of us. When we begin to move, our visitors begin the frenetic and hopeless search for seatbelts. I'm grinning now. Inches separate our van from the ones on all sides of us, and all eyes foreign to this overwhelming scene are wide. If horns could decide who moved first, our driver would clearly be in the lead, but we're boxed in. Our driver inches forward until we block traffic. We're given a gap to squeeze through and we're on the way to the hotel. Our visitors are quietly shaking their heads. Someone, unable to take it anymore, yells at the driver to turn the music down as Tony

Orlando and Dawn sing the obnoxious, "Tie a Yellow Ribbon 'Round the Old Oak Tree", but he can't hear them. The music is too loud.

People are everywhere — thousands of them —and it's after midnight. Traffic momentarily thins out and our driver turns into Jimmie Johnson. Substituting the horn for brakes, we swerve in and out of traffic – one visitor holds her breath, another hyperventilates. One passenger lets out a muffled scream as we weave through traffic, ignoring every driving rule ever taught. Roy Orbison is now crooning "Only The Lonely" so loudly that nobody even attempts to speak. The twenty-five minutes to the hotel seem surreal. People are sleeping in the median – whole families. A man is vomiting on the sidewalk. A man pulling a wooden cart filled with trash is blocking the left lane of traffic. A pedestrian struggles to escape the grip of two girls who are pulling him to the door of a "Disco". Two men are urinating on a wall. Our driver ignores a policeman signaling him to stop.

Small children beg for coins at the traffic lights, and our visitors discover that they don't yet have pesos. A dollar bill is pushed through the rear-opening window to a small, scruffy boy with homemade shoes. He dropped the bill and was immediately knocked down by an older girl, who emerged, grinning, from a brief scuffle with the bill above her head. A dangerous looking man with a rag tied onto his head approaches the van at the next stoplight. He's apparently selling bottled water. Our visitors shift nervously, trying to avoid direct eye contact with him, but he knocks continuously on the window until we begin to move. Two vendors approach us at the next light; the one on the driver's side is selling cigarettes and hard candies, the one on the passenger side is still trying to get rid of yesterday's newspapers. Our driver unrolled his window to buy a single cigarette and a small girl selling strings of fragrant flowers climbs his door and sticks her head inside to get a better look at us. The driver pushes her and she stumbles backwards for several steps before recovering her balance. She smiles and waves at us as we drive away. We arrive at our hotel just in time – "Rock Lobster" by the B-52's blasts through the speakers as we unload our bags.

Our visitors are given keys to their hotel rooms and they quickly head upstairs for some much needed rest, but in order to sleep they'll need to tune out the sounds of horns and jackhammers on the street below – Manila never sleeps. The hot shower feels great, and it will be last they enjoy until they leave. They can't sleep – their bodies tell them it's only 1:30 PM and they napped on the last flight out of sheer exhaustion. They enjoy their final night of air conditioning, wondering what lies ahead. Life as they know it is about to change.

But blessed are your eyes because they see, and your ears because they hear. – Matthew 13:16

Chapter Four Discussion Questions

1. Make a list of at least ten adjectives that you believe describe the place you're going to. Compare your list with other team members.

2. Are you sensitive to foul odors? How will you overcome them? (Hint: I carry a small container of Tiger Balm® in my backpack to sniff when odors become too thick.)

3. Are there any specific team instructions about what information to include (or not to include) on immigration and customs forms?

4. Do you have the address and phone number of your host missionary to carry with you?

5. Do you know the name and location of the hotel where you'll be staying at upon arrival?

6. Have you considered bringing along earplugs or noise canceling headphones to permit you to have peace in the midst of cacophony?

7. How will you deal with persistent street vendors or beggars? Has your team established any policy regarding giving to beggars?

Mandatory Machetes

Some cultural differences are subtle, almost unnoticeable, such as clothing or hairstyles. A meal at McDonald's here in the Philippines would be much the same as in the US except that the table will be cleared by the restaurant staff instead of expecting you, as the customer, to throw away your own trash. Food quality is much the same, but you'll notice other items, such as chicken and rice or spaghetti on the menu. You may notice that the staff here in the Philippines seems to be more cheerful and better trained than in the US, and you'd be correct in that assessment; fast food employment, particularly with international chains, is a great job here in the Philippines. These are coveted jobs and employee turnover is minimal.

But there are some shocking cultural differences that you'll encounter as you spend time here. Any student found with a knife at school in the US would be immediately suspended or expelled. The incident might even appear in the local news. Here in the Aurora Province, students are *required* to bring machetes to school. The teachers specify that they are to be big ones, and insist that they're sharp. Students are expected to cut the grass with their machetes.

They dig weeds, perform school beautification and manage community gardens, and they are *punished if they fail to bring* their knife to school!

Large warehouse stores like Sam's Club ® and COSTCO® appeal to Americans. We receive discounts for buying things in bulk. It may take us two years to use a drum of detergent or a barrel of pickles, but we save money when we buy in bulk. There's less packaging involved, so we believe we're helping the environment as we cart home shampoo in gallon-sized containers. Contrast our buying habits with the Philippines (and most of the world). Most of the people in my neighborhood have no refrigerators so they purchase nothing that requires refrigeration. Leftover food remains out until it is eaten. There's very little storage space and people can't afford to purchase tomorrow's food, so they focus only on what they need for today – typically thinking of only the next meal. Instead of buying a gallon of cooking oil, they bring a baby food jar to the corner store and buy just enough oil to cook the next meal. Salt, pepper, garlic, chili peppers, sugar, and coffee are repackaged for single servings. Bay leaves come three to a package. Shampoo is purchased in small, single use packets. Filipinos shop exactly the opposite way that we do, buying only what is needed for today, in as small a quantity as possible.

I've always understood the concept of 'return for deposit' bottles. In fact, I think that the same concept should be applied to aluminum cans, glass jars, plastic milk jugs, cardboard boxes and other recyclable containers. But 'return for deposit' simply doesn't apply here in the Philippines because absolutely nothing is wasted. Someone will use a discarded bottle. I didn't realize this until my household goods arrived here from Seattle. After we emptied the truck I began to unpack the boxes. These were strong, triple-walled boxes that held no value whatsoever to me – I considered them as clutter and I cut them apart with a case cutter and immediately burned them in my back yard. The neighbors I hired to help me unload the truck, watched quietly; nobody was willing to speak up and tell me that I was an idiot. They watched me destroy the highest quality boxes they had ever seen, perfect for lining the inside of their walls to protect their families from the rain and insects. It was many months later that my mistake sank in. While attending our weekly men's breakfast, hosted in a different home each week, I discovered cardboard linings inside every home I visited. I still feel foolish.

We were stuck in Manila traffic and carrying six too many passengers when the air conditioner of our Ford Cortina died. I was feeling claustrophobic and overheating when I suggested that we buy some soft drinks. Our driver jumped out of the car and ran into a small grocery store, returning with eleven plastic baggies filled with *Coca Cola®.* They transferred the contents from bottles to plastic bags so that we wouldn't drive off with the valuable bottles. A straw stuck out the top of each bag. I was amazed at the ingenuity, yet was also a bit clumsy in handling my baggie, spilling a portion onto my lap. Nobody here would be surprised to be handed a beverage-filled plastic bag with a straw in it. They expect it. As a visitor here you need to expect the unexpected.

I was appalled as each of our passengers pitched his or her plastic bag to the street from our car as we finished our drinks. I discovered that "littering" is an unfamiliar term here. Honestly, they had never heard the word. The Philippines is a nation of litterbugs. Tons of plastic float down the rivers into the ocean. A boat ride on Manila bay reveals layers of suspended garbage. The city of Manila floods after heavy rainstorms because plastic bags clog up all the drains. There's simply a very different paradigm here regarding trash, and environmental education is just now beginning to creep into the public school system. Vacant lots continue to accumulate garbage and become a dumping place for the neighbors. There are no public trash receptacles, so people throw garbage wherever they wish.

I watched a truck driver drain his oil into the Malupa River, and thought to myself that this would be considered a criminal act in the

US. Later I spotted other drivers doing the same thing. Draining their oil into the river is what they've been *taught* to do. Environmental stewardship simply doesn't exist. People dynamite the reefs to catch fish. Some use cyanide to poison the fish, killing the reefs just as thoroughly as the dynamite blasts. Car batteries and electrodes are used to shock fresh water critters, and anything large enough to see is harvested. There is a total logging ban in effect, yet groups of men with chain saws take as many trees from the forest as they are able.

Common knowledge here contains some odd things. For instance, getting wet in the rain is responsible for fevers and colds. It was explained to me that evaporation from the soil delivers contaminants into your system as it rises from the dirt. Everyone here insists that cold beverages are responsible for sore throats. I've stopped trying to explain germs and viruses. In fact, I spend very little energy defending the way we think in America. Thankfully, that's not my purpose here. Just because something is different doesn't mean it's inferior. I have no desire to see the Philippines become like America. My desire, implanted deep in my heart by the Lord, is to see Filipinos commit themselves to a life of service to our Lord, Jesus Christ.

Finally brothers, whatever is true, whatever is noble, whatever is right, whatever is pure, whatever is lovely, whatever is admirable - if anything is excellent or praiseworthy - think about such things. - Philippians 4:8

Chapter Five Discussion Questions

1. Have you been made aware of any cultural taboos in the nation you are visiting?

   a. Are you aware of things that are forbidden to be carried into the country?

   b. Are you educated with regards to cultural differences such as clothing that might be considered 'provocative?'

   c. Have you been alerted to any social mistakes, such as a woman conversing with men (or vice versa) during social events?

   d. Is it forbidden or acceptable to touch a child?

   e. Are any parts of the body (head or feet in particular) considered sacred or filthy to touch?

   f. Are any there any innocent gestures considered offensive in your host culture?

2. Will you defend 'the way we do things back home' when you find people doing something familiar, but in a strangely new way?

3. Can you distinguish between mere cultural differences (that don't require changing) and practices that are an affront to God?

6 Collide with nothing

Our bus driver is a heavyset, mustachioed man with tattoos that extend from under his crisp, white, short-sleeved shirt all the way to his fingers. He apparently can't read because there are four signs posted inside the bus that state clearly, "No Smoking Permitted", yet he lights each new cigarette with the previous. The television set above his head is playing a Jon Claude Van Damme film and he's far more interested in the movie than the road in front of us. He's straining backward in his seat, standing at times, to see the video. Nobody else seems alarmed that he's watching the movie along with them as we snake along the dirt mountain road.

An ancient, rust-colored bus suddenly bursts around a tight curve in front of us into our lane. It's leaning at an angle that physics doesn't allow, barreling downhill and tipping into our lane just 100 feet in front of us. The top of the bus is filled with baskets, sacks of rice and terrified passengers, who are now scrambling, climbing to the high side of the bus. One is carrying a baby! The wheels on the mountain-side of the bus leave the ground, but, miraculously, the weight of the climbing passengers shifts the bus back onto the ground and it rights itself just in time to miss us. Our driver never slowed down. He may not have seen it happen as he was texting someone on his cell phone.

I pray for our passengers as we traverse through the mountains, especially when our driver is in a hurry and accelerates in all the wrong places. A terrible D' Liner bus crash killed more than 40 people last year when it plunged sixty feet into a ravine in the Sierra Madre mountains on the way to Baler. The driver lived, so they blamed faulty brakes. It's hard to pinpoint a single cause for an accident here – there are just too many causes to count. It could have been the horrible brakes that wail and screech and emit foul-smelling smoke for much of the time through the mountains. Maybe the bald tires contributed to the crash. Hopefully the driver wasn't eating, smoking, watching a movie and texting when it happened.

Once we leave the mountains I pray for everything in front of our bus. A tricycle (motorcycle with sidecar) with nine or ten school kids pulls in front of us from a side street. Its driver never even looked left before pulling in front of us. The bus driver blasts his air horn and brakes hard. Packages fly down from the small overhead compartments. We remain behind the tricycle, smoke swirling steadily from its tailpipe, for more than a kilometer, moving at seven or eight miles per hour. Our driver decides to take advantage of a 40-

meter gap in oncoming traffic, and horn blaring, swerves into oncoming traffic. Before he's completely around the tricycle he pulls back into the right lane, forcing the trike with the kids off the road.

The drive likens a high-speed race-car video game as the roads swerve and curve and bump. In fact, there should be a video game that depicts driving here. The most popular means of public transportation in the Philippines is called a Jeepney. They are extended versions of Willys World War II quarter ton jeeps with bench seats that face one another. A jeepney with no tail lights stops suddenly in front of us to let a passenger get off. We swerve around him into oncoming traffic, forcing yet another tricycle off the road. An old woman snatches her grandchild out of the way an instant before the tricycle would have run him over. It's like they're part of an orchestrated dance, but I know better. I'd feel more comfortable if it was choreographed, but I've witnessed too many missteps in this tango to feel anything but numb as we race down the narrow streets.

Kids play a game to see who can get closest to the moving traffic without getting hit. Suicidal dogs lie in the roadway. Rice, for almost two kilometers, covers half of the road (which is only half a road in the first place.) Logs are placed in the road in one neighborhood to slow the traffic. Other communities erect metal barricades to slow traffic. There are COMELEC checkpoints (near election time to check passengers for weapons). There are military checkpoints. There are DENR (Department of Energy and Natural Resources) checkpoints to make sure no illegally harvested logs pass. Drivers barely slow down at these checkpoints; they're just another road obstacle, navigated at the highest speed possible.

A small cart pulled by an aging water buffalo slows our bus to a near standstill. Moments later we accelerate past him, full throttle, to maximum velocity, then decelerate to a walking pace again behind a bicycle with a side cart. An eighteen wheeled truck is coming toward us in our lane. He's flashing his headlights, which basically means "I'm coming through." The only thing that really matters is vehicle size. A car, two tricycles and an oversized jeepney move onto the shoulder to escape the huge oncoming truck. Our bus driver is flashing our lights back at the truck. The truck driver re-enters his lane, which is filled with drying rice, and the two drivers honk at one another and smile as we pass. A tricycle in front of us with a ten-year-old driver pulls a sudden u-turn. Sometimes a passenger will signal with his foot. Other times the driver will turn his head to the left, but most of the time there's no warning. The child driver stops in the road as a passenger jumps off to retrieve her sandal that fell off during his maneuver. The child seated in the isle across from me vomits into a plastic bag.

Our bus conductor becomes animated, pointing out an oncoming bus to our driver. Our driver shifts to the center of the road, as does the oncoming bus. They are playing chicken and loving it. I'm not. At the very last second both drivers swerve to avoid a head-on collision. The driver's side-view mirrors meet, clicking together without breaking. Most of the passengers are sleeping, but the few who just witnessed our near death experience are more amused than outraged. We race up behind a motorcycle with a man and three children on it. Our driver moves close enough to them to make them disappear from my view – and I'm seated in the second seat!

We've been on the road for four hours and have killed a slow-moving dog and a chicken that zigged when he should have zagged. It was likely an imported Texas rooster used for cockfighting – native chickens are too clever to get hit by traffic here. We stopped in the mountains to allow an oncoming jeep and a tricycle to navigate past us in the single lane of mud. Our driver wasn't able to wait the extra two seconds to let the tricycle clear our bus, and collided with the tricycle as we began to move. He broke the cardinal rule here: collide with nothing. In fact, it is the only rule here. Our driver and conductor hop quickly out of the bus and accuse the tricycle driver of moving too slowly, which would seem to be no offense anywhere else. They check the paint on the side of the bus, then curse the driver of the disabled tricycle, its wheel bent in half, as they climb back into the bus shaking their heads. We drive away – no authorities involved, no accident report, no justice.

If you should, unfortunately, collide with another vehicle, there's a universal rule regarding blame – the largest vehicle is automatically at fault. When a bus and a jeepney collide, the bus is at fault. When a jeepney and a passenger car collide, the jeepney is at fault. If a car hits a tricycle, the car is at fault. And if any of them hits a pedestrian, God save them. I was told, "Go to the nearest police station and turn yourself in, but DO NOT STOP to check on the condition of any pedestrian that you've run into. Neighbors and enraged family members will chop you into small pieces with machetes." Gratefully, I've never been put in that situation.

You rarely encounter them in the Aurora Province, but Land Transportation Officers appear in clusters, like uniformed jackals, in population centers. They don't investigate accidents. And they rarely direct traffic. They just pull over traffic, looking for reasons to write citations. They prefer professional drivers who can't afford to surrender their licenses. If they can't find a legitimate reason for a citation, they'll fabricate a reason. All they want is some money, and drivers here are quick to offer to buy them breakfast. If you have no driver's license, or if your vehicle is not properly registered, no problem, you'll just need to buy a more expensive breakfast for them - and, perhaps, lunch and dinner. I've never witnessed a confiscated vehicle or seen a driver who didn't drive away in the same vehicle after being stopped by the LTO. As long as a driver is cooperative, it's certain that a deal will be found to make the citation go away.

Teenagers from America love the freedom here. They don't need a license or insurance to drive (and people will offer to let them!) They can ride inside a vehicle if they feel conventional, but most will choose to ride on top or standing on the bumpers and running boards as we motor down the street. Some have even opted to sit on the hood as we motor down the road. Most prefer riding on the tricycles because they are novel - they've never seen them before - and they can still ride on the top or stand on the back of them. I would like to advise team leaders to set safety expectations *before* they arrive in country – it's much harder get them into the seats after they've experienced the exhilaration of surfing on the top of a moving trike. If seat belts are part of your safety precautions, bring some along and we'll have somebody install them for your use.

And the peace of God, which transcends all understanding, will guard your hearts and your minds in Christ Jesus. - Philippians 4:7

Chapter Six Discussion Questions

1. Who is making your travel arrangements from the airport?

2. Will your team be separated during any of your travel?

3. Will you or any of your teammates be expected to drive in your host nation?

    a. If so, does your insurance cover you in that country?

    b. How will you deal with police officers who approach you and expect a bribe?

    c. Are you familiar with the language or road signs?

4. What is your team policy about riding atop vehicles, hanging off the back, or riding anyplace not considered a *passenger area* of the vehicle?

7 Critters

The condition of most dogs in my neighborhood would send their owners to jail in the U.S. for animal cruelty. Many canines are malnourished with ribs exposed like meat in a grocery store. These animals are covered in fleas and mange, appear pinkish with most of the hair on their bodies long gone. Some have ugly scars from fighting with other dogs or perhaps where they've been cut by an angry drunk. Some are missing legs. One has a scrotal tumor the size of a large coconut that he drags around the neighborhood. He was here last night. These animals have been mistreated and are dangerous – don't try to pet them unless you want to undergo a painful series of rabies shots.

"Boots" was a dog who 'materialized' at our home every day. He spent more time here than elsewhere, but he didn't belong to us - I'm not sure he could have belonged to anybody. He sported a huge machete scar across his back, and was quite aggressive. He didn't just bark when people were near my fence, he attacked them ferociously and relentlessly. I witnessed Boots attack a worker mending my neighbor's fence, lunging repeatedly at the frustrated young man. Boots was clearly trying to bite him and he showed his teeth and snarled until the worker backed away, unable to turn his back on Boots for even a moment. Dogs like Boots will confront you as you walk through neighborhoods; know in advance that these dogs do, in fact, bite. Boots often growled and showed his teeth to our other dogs, particularly when food was involved. At the same time, Boots was hungry for attention, coming to me to be petted each time I worked in the garden. I think he slept in the field near our home, and was always alert when he was around even though he showed affection towards me. My next door neighbor captured Boots and sold him as food to a group of drunks.

The public health clinic in Baler, our provincial capital, has veterinarians on staff. We contacted them when our female black lab, Badette, was dying from a uterine infection and they came to our house on three consecutive days to inject her with antibiotics. They told us that we're the only family they've encountered who's willing to unhand money to heal a dog (even though our total cost was a whopping six U.S. dollars!) Dogs aren't pets here; they're like livestock – a future food supply. One of our pastors tried to convince a neighbor to provide one of his new puppies to become the main dish at a birthday party. Dogs = food.

The veterinarian who came to our house to treat Badette brought along 'anti-rabies' vaccine for my other two dogs. If people know that you've injected the dogs they won't eat them. I'm told it ruins the taste. The veterinarian told us that when they arrive in a neighborhood that people actually hide their dogs to prevent them from receiving anti-rabies shots. It's also rumored that the inoculations cause the dogs to have mange. Dogs are everywhere here. They bark, breed, fight, mark their territories, and share their fleas, mange and rabies. Two people in my neighborhood have died from rabies since I moved here.

I have a doctor friend who described a recent patient who arrived at his clinic suffering from rabies. He was already past the point of no return and was advised to go home and prepare for death. He was given the option to travel to Cabanatuan or Manila and spend lots of money and die elsewhere, and he opted to save the money and die at home just 48 hours later. I don't want to go into details, but dying from rabies is a gruesome death. And getting treated for rabies, once bitten, is no picnic either. You may be placed on 'international hold' for medical reasons and not permitted to leave the Philippines until the twenty-one day treatment is completed.

Americans are horrified to witness small children play with animals here. One visiting missionary tried to disrupt a game of frog tag, a game that involves preschool children throwing a large toad at one another. The kids were baffled by the request to stop playing. We've watched one of our pastor's sons choke and squeeze the life out of more than one bird. There's simply a different standard when it comes to treatment of animals here.

I advise visitors to avoid touching any kind of *critter*. All cats have claws here – they couldn't survive without them. Not many cats survive due to the rampant dog population here, and those that do survive are beyond tough – they're ferocious. The toads around my yard secrete a poison that is absorbed through skin. Several snake species here are deadly, and the Philippine cobra is aggressive. The Philippines has the world's largest and smallest species of bat, and, thankfully, they are plentiful enough to keep the insect population in check.

Exotic pets are common here. You'll find monkeys tethered by a chain to a bamboo pole at some houses. The initial reaction by most visitors is to move closer to the cute monkeys as they rarely see monkeys up close. You've been warned - they have very sharp teeth and, if you get within reach, you'll discover that they move faster than flyweight boxers. Some will spit at you or urinate on you as you walk underneath them. Others do even worse things. There are reasons that pet monkeys haven't proliferated throughout homes in the US. Never trust a monkey.

We have a species of monitor lizard here called 'bayawak.' They are carnivores of the first order. They move like lightning and sport razor-sharp teeth, so you'd be wasting your time to try to capture one. And we'd get to test your travel insurance if you managed to corner one. I believe we've lost some puppies to bayawak, thinking that they were taken by a thief. Maybe the Lord will reveal that information to me as we review my life. When on the mission field, leave all critters alone!

A righteous man cares for the needs of his animals, but the kindest acts of the wicked are cruel - Proverbs 12:10

Chapter Seven Discussion Questions

1. Curb your love for animals and pledge not to touch any living creature!

2. Report any animal scratches or bites immediately.

3. How will you respond if you witness animal cruelty?

4. If you need to ride an animal, are you prepared to do so safely?

5. What will you do if confronted by snarling dogs?

◁(8)▷ **Your check should clear in 60 days**

American Express commercials want you to know how vulnerable you are when you travel with cash in your pocket – especially overseas.   They use the tag line: "American Express traveler's checks – don't leave home without them." And they have a well-reasoned appeal — cash that is lost or stolen is simply gone, but traveler's lost or stolen traveler's checks can be replaced. What they fail to tell you is that nobody will accept a traveler's check in the Philippines. Businesses throughout the Philippines have been repeatedly duped by sophisticated forgeries, so if you come here with traveler's checks, you'll be going home with all of them.

Filipino clerks first chuckle when you suggest payment by personal check, suppressing wild laughter, then they grin so broadly that you notice their lack of proper dental care. Their laugh becomes audible when they see that it's a check from abroad. Let's put it in perspective. Imagine that you run a small roadside fruit stand in near Farmville, Georgia when a man who is unable to speak a single word of English comes to the counter. He points to dozens of items he wants to purchase and you stack each of them on the countertop as he points to them. He then pulls out a checkbook (despite the "ABSOLUTELY NO CHECKS" sign hanging from the front of the table) and writes you a check in the proper amount from the National Bank of Slavanka. You have no way to verify the check's authenticity, so you point at your sign and politely indicate that you can't accept his check. He shows his irritation, rolling his eyes and signaling you to wait while he finds another form of payment. He now produces a Slavankian Express Traveler's Check, with the amount of $500 neatly printed on the front in Slavankanese. His temper flares when you indicate that you can't accept his traveler's check. "*What!? I can't believe this*!" he bellows loudly in harsher Slavankanese tones. "*Everyone accepts Slavankian Express – these are good anywhere!*" You have no idea what he said, but the tone indicates that he's unhappy. Even if you could accept the traveler's check, you couldn't make change for the $500 amount. In a huff, he whips out a MasterCard from his wallet and pitches it onto the fruit counter. You shake your head to indicate that his plastic won't work either. He just stares at you quietly now, with his mouth open in disbelief. Then, his displeasure clearly on display, he snatches 28 Slavankian drachmas from his pocket to pay you in cash. By now you're pretty sure that you're the victim of some sort of hidden camera reality show and begin looking around for the film crew as you push his drachma back across the counter, explaining that you accept only US dollars. He then explodes as he grabs his cash off the table and storms back to his car, yelling loudly over his shoulder the entire way. He slams his car door, revs his engine loudly, then shoots gravel at you as his tires rip up your parking area. Why, in rural Georgia, wouldn't he have US currency with him?

The same holds true for us when we travel to remote regions of other countries; we need to be prepared to do business in the local currency. Most businesses don't accept credit cards, can't exchange dollars easily, and are unwilling to accept the risks associated with checks. Getting loud and ugly with managers damages our ministry, so we simply need to be knowledgeable about foreign currencies prior to leaving our home country. Or well in advance of the trip. You can exchange money before you leave the airport, but will get a better exchange rate at the hotel or one of the many money-changers in Manila. Exchange all that you think you'll need before returning to Manila, but no more than you think you'll require for the entire trip. The money changers, including at the airport, won't buy back your pesos, so unless you plan to bring it home as souvenirs, exchange only what you intend to spend.

In the Philippines, you won't be able to exchange blemished American currency. Blemished is defined as bills that have been stamped, written on, torn, or just worn. Even a visible crease in the fold of a bill will make it unacceptable, so make sure that you bring only 'clean' bills for exchange. Most money exchanges don't want small bills either, and only accept denominations of twenty dollars or higher.

Your host missionary may be willing to exchange your one, five and ten dollar bills, or exchange a bill that is deemed to be blemished and is unacceptable to the money changers. But understand that you are doing them a disservice when you leave them with money that can't be converted into the local currency; they will be stuck with those bills until they return to the United States. And if your host missionary is willing to convert your dollars into the local currency, please don't make it a daily thing. We recently experienced a brother who changed his dollars into pesos one dollar at a time. He requested another dollar's worth of pesos often and sometimes four or five times a day.

On her way from Manila to the Province Sandra, a missionary from Virginia, decided to buy a soft drink when our bus stopped for fuel. The store clerk told Sandra that the price of the drink was twelve pesos; she then reached deep into her backpack and pulled out a quart sized plastic bag filled with money. She peeled off a thousand peso bill and gave it to the poor girl behind the counter, who explained that she didn't have change for such a large bill (almost $20.00).

Sandra returned to her backpack and produced a small fanny pack,

pulling out another large wad of bills. Four men eating at a nearby

table watched her intently. One pulled out his cell phone and began

texting, his eyes never left Sandra the entire time. We need to be

intelligent about carrying money. Carry what you think you'll need in

an accessible location, like your front pocket. Hide larger amounts in

a money belt (which, by the way, is supposed to be worn inside of

your clothing.) Divide it up into three places, making it less likely that

you'll lose it all in the unlikely event of a robbery.

Hopefully you'll never need to go to a Philippine bank.

Americans have been spoiled by ATM machines and drive-up tellers

and would be furious if a transaction took thirty minutes to complete.

Things are very different in the Philippines (and likely most other third

world countries.) When we first moved to the Philippines there wasn't

a bank in the Aurora Province willing to accept our personal checks.

None of the banks offered dollar accounts – the only currency

permitted was pesos. This forced us to go to Cabanatuan City once

each month to deposit a check with Philippine National Bank. It

typically took around 30 days for our check to 'clear' (even though our

credit union statement showed that it cleared in three days.) We felt

vulnerable traveling through the mountains carrying large amounts of cash. We praise God that we now have dollar accounts available in Baler, about twenty minutes from home, but our checks now take 60-90 days to 'clear'. If you happen to need banking services while you're here, be prepared for a shock.

Most banks employ uniformed guards who carry shotguns and side arms. Our bank in Baler has three of them. They help seat customers and establish the pecking order for clients. The first time I went to the bank in Baler it appeared as though people making deposits moved more quickly than people needing to conduct other transactions. Two clerks were trying to service a waiting room filled with over a hundred people and the average wait exceeded two hours. Three other tellers sat near the rear of the bank laughing and joking the entire time I waited. Once we made it to the counter and the teller learned that we wanted to open up an account with thousands of dollars, the manager was summoned and he quickly sent out for coffee and snacks. He's instructed the guards to remember our faces and to seat us in his office and serve us snacks when we arrive at the bank. And that's how it is here – people of means are a privileged class and don't have to wait in lines.

When I deposited our money in the bank here I didn't know that the Philippine equivalent of the FDIC only insures 100,000 pesos in the event that the bank fails. That's just over two thousand dollars.

We had several thousand deposited with the Most Rural Provincial Bank (not their real name) and they became over-extended. They had plenty of land holdings, but no available cash. When I tried to remove a few hundred dollars I was told to return the following week. Then I was told to return the week after that. Soon it was clear that our money was not available. They began to make deals with us. "Does your car need to be painted? We have a client who owes us money who can paint your car for you." That was over five years ago and we still have money in that bank that we can't retrieve. At least it's drawing interest. The Most Rural Provincial Bank has never declared bankruptcy, so the government insurance isn't an option. As Christians we don't resort to threats or behave rudely because we can't get what we expect (even though it's what any reasonable person should expect.) We simply pray.

Let's go back to credit cards for a minute. Please know that if you find a vendor to accept a credit card that you will be charged an additional 4% on top of your purchase as a "credit card processing fee." Merchants in the US absorb the credit card fees as part of doing business, understanding that they'd lose business if they didn't accept them. Merchants in the Philippines view them as a necessary evil and will permit you to use your credit card, but they make it quite difficult. When I purchased a computer by credit card in Cabanatuan they needed to fax copies of my picture ID to some approval authority and they actually took my photo and fingerprinted me at the store counter!

To my knowledge we've never experienced theft from any of our visitors who have come to Aurora. But we are cautious, and advise all visitors not to bring along excessive amounts of money. We also suggest that they carry a backpack for their valuables rather than leaving cash, cameras, laptops, etc in an unattended hotel room. Don't consider bringing along expensive jewelry; you can live without your diamond for two weeks. This includes expensive watches. You'll find that you won't need to check on the time as nothing here happens at the appointed time. I stopped wearing a watch in 1999 because it was only a source of frustration.

Except for snacks and small expenses you shouldn't need to have much money while here on a mission trip. We suggest no more than two hundred dollars as spending money, and you'll likely go home with half of that.

One last thing regarding money: bring enough. It's bad form to run out of money, and be forced to borrow more from your team members or your host. This happens too frequently, particularly with youth. Travel with sufficient funds to last until you return home, and live within your means so that it lasts the entire trip. And understand that your credit card, ATM card, checks or other forms of 'money' are

not the same as cash. You'll need cash, converted into the national

currency, in order to buy anything here.

Wisdom is supreme; therefore get wisdom. Though it costs all you have, get understanding. Proverbs 4:7

Chapter Eight Discussion Questions

1. How much cash do you plan to carry with you?

2. Where will you convert your money into the local currency?

3. Are the bills you plan to carry clean and unblemished?

4. Do you have a money belt or another place to hide your money in more than one location?

5. Have you been advised regarding the use of debit or credit cards where you are going?

6. Is there any reason you would need to cash a check while on your mission trip? If not, leave the checkbook at home.

7. How will you keep your expensive camera, notebook computer, or other portable electronic devices safe?

8. How can you minimize the possibility of being targeted by thieves?

Ant eggs

If you're an adventurous eater, the Philippine islands provide some culinary options that you'd be well-served to avoid. My neighbors are aware that I'm quite adventurous when it comes to food, so they bring me samples of various and unknown plants and animals. And I test everything they bring to me. I was once served a bowl of ant eggs, which tasted like smoke. There was no other discernable flavor, I stopped with a single spoonful and was grateful that I did. Five minutes later my face was swollen with huge red, itchy blotches. Hives broke out on my neck, chest and back, and breathing became difficult. I quickly took two Benadryl capsules, laid down and prayed as my breathing became quite labored. It took more than an hour for my breathing to normalize and for the itching to stop. Imagine what would have happened if I had enjoyed the taste of the ant eggs and eaten the entire bowl!

People eat the mangy, nasty dogs that you see roaming the neighborhood. They chop them into small cubes and stew them with vinegar and spices, and (I hate to admit this) they taste quite good. It's now against the law to butcher and eat dogs. That law was enacted in order to appease the international community – but it's never been enforced here in Aurora. Since it's no longer legal to eat dog, I'll find my culinary adventures eating other 'delicacies.'

Some people (suffering from some childhood food substitution disorder) have voiced concern about the food that they'll be served, fearing that they'll be surreptitiously served dog disguised as pork or eel disguised as fish. Oftentimes, they'll end up eating rat meat they were told was chicken. Fear not. Filipinos will tell you honestly what you're being served, especially if it's something unusual. We order our meals from the *resort* where we stay and the kitchen staff provides us with a variety of fish, chicken, and pork, with vegetables that Americans recognize. They also serve plenty of fresh fruit: mangoes, pineapple, papaya, watermelon and bananas and pleasantly, rice! Rice is served at breakfast, lunch, and supper.

Andrew Zimmern, host of Bizarre Foods, is a chunky bald guy who travels around the world eating unusual and exotic food. You can view his visit to the Philippines on YouTube. He managed to eat live 'woody-flavored' mangrove worms as they were pulled out of trees. He gave a thumbs-up when he ate a balut – a nearly hatched fermented duck egg. He enjoyed a cricket stir-fry, deep-fried frog stuffed with pork, roasted baby chicks, and ice cream from a purple root called ube eaten on bread. There are things here that Andrew didn't eat, such as the foul-smelling durian fruit (although he tried.) I didn't notice him purchase any skewered chicken heads, feet, or intestines, which are cooked over open coals and sold everywhere. Nor did I notice him try diniguan, a fried pork blood mixture. There's enough bizarre food here to shoot another five or six episodes, and I'm quite sure that you'll see Andrew Zimmern back in the Philippines for an encore.

The reason I'm even writing this chapter is to dissuade you (yes, youth pastor, I'm talking to you) from eating anything that could take you out of service for a few days. It's happened before. There's a gene that's activated in some young men that compels them to show others that they can eat anything. These were the same kids eating paste or bugs in your elementary class and grinning when you became repulsed by the act. We've had visitors with this gene and the consequential need to eat bizarre things to gross out their comrades. More than half ended up with diarrhea, known here as LBM (loose bowel movement.) One case is believed to have been dysentery. The sickness is temporary, but may prevent you from fulfilling the purpose that God planned for you on your trip. A day or two of LBM and vomiting may only reduce your effectiveness, but it's a shame to miss what the Lord is doing with the rest of the team. If you feel compelled to eat something strange, buy it and bring it home with you.

There's the other extreme that also needs to be addressed – people who are so picky about what they eat that they refuse to eat anything that is prepared for the team. They don't eat chicken, don't like rice, can't stand vegetables, hate fish, gag on fruits, and feel sick at the smell of all the above. They retreat to their room during mealtimes to eat granola bars, chips, cookies, or whatever they packed to bring along on the trip. I have a problem with these people for three reasons:

(1) They insult their hosts who prepared them food;

(2) They miss out on important mealtime fellowship;

(3) They weaken as the trip progresses and cause alarm for other team members.

I'm not sure what they expected to eat while visiting a remote jungle region, but McDonald's, Pizza Hut, and Taco Bell, are not an option here. Don't expect hamburgers, French fries, milk shakes, pizza (or anything that requires an oven), ice cream, or cheese. Just be open to new foods and tastes. The unfamiliar adds to the heightened sense of being on mission.

We've also hosted people who have blood sugar issues, gluten allergies, sodium concerns, or of whom were allergic to MSG.

As long as you identify your dietary needs, we can help you avoid foods that make you twitch, bloat, or bark at the moon. Don't wait until you arrive to tell your host. It's important to make sure that they include your needs as they shop to prepare the food that they'll serve you upon your arrival. Otherwise, you'll watch your team eat barbeque pork sticks with macaroni salad as you eat another granola bar.

Repeat after me: new food is fun, new food is fun, new food is fun! It really is!

Of these you may eat any kind of locust, katydid, cricket or grasshopper.
- Leviticus 11:22

Chapter Nine Discussion Questions

1. How will you respond when you are offered food that doesn't appeal to you?

2. Do you have any food allergies that you need to make known?

3. Has your team established any rules regarding meal-time etiquette?

4. If dared to eat some grotesque, foul-smelling delicacy, will you resist?

5. If you are considered to be a picky eater, how will you overcome your food preferences to join others at mealtimes and *eat the food that has been prepared for your team?*

6. Are you willing to try new foods?

10 Lepers!

I recently visited with an elderly man at his home and noticed that his hand was severely disfigured as I shook it. The damage was quite severe and I asked him about it, expecting to hear the story of an industrial accident or, because of his age, I considered it might have been an injury from the Second World War. To my horror, I discovered that this disfigurement was caused by *leprosy!* I was pretty sure that I'd heard it right, but asked our pastor to translate the conversation for me, and it was confirmed – *leprosy*! I don't remember much of our conversation after that, all I could think was 'God help me, I've been touched by a leper!' I envisioned my final years of ministry taking place on Culion Island (a leper colony established during the US occupation of the Philippines) spending my final days counting my fingers and toes.

Immediately after the visit I returned home and scrubbed my hands, then squirted half a bottle of hand sanitizer on them. I scoured my hands in the same way I washed them after an accidental dog bite from our yellow lab during a local rabies outbreak. Both times I scrubbed until my hands were raw. I knew a week after the dog bite that I didn't have rabies, but I have no clue when my fingers might begin to fall off as a result of my encounter with the leper.

Many of our teams go door-to-door while they are here, and there's no telling what sort of medical conditions that we could encounter. Contagious diseases that are uncommon back home, such as tuberculosis, are quite commonplace here. But as ambassadors for Christ, we don't avoid visits to infected people or show them any less love because of their afflictions. And, please embrace this concept: *we don't sanitize in front of them*!

One of our visitors, a cheerful young woman who emanated Jesus, accompanied me and two female translators as we visited house-to-house. She was full of hugs and smiles and was truly a joy to be around, radiant in her faith. It was likely unconscious behavior, but immediately after each hug or handshake she would reach into her backpack and squirt some hand sanitizer into her palm to cleanse away any chance cooties from the encounter. "I'm pleased to meet you", – squirt. "It's been a pleasure talking with you," – squirt. Our translators began to look at one another each time the hand sanitizer was drawn from the backpack. After several visits it caused them to giggle.

I know that Jesus didn't carry hand sanitizer with him during his ministry, yet he touched and healed a leper (Mark 1:40-45.) At that time leprosy was incurable by human means, and even if you didn't catch the disease, you would be considered ceremoniously unclean if you touched a person with leprosy. It's significant to note in this passage that Jesus actually touched the leper, which was not the case in many other miracles. It was a deliberate touch, designed to show compassion and let both the man healed and all who witnessed understand the nature of Jesus. He demonstrated to the priests that compassion trumps 'ceremoniously clean.' He also demonstrated to the leper that all are worthy of his love. We, too, need to be willing to touch lepers.

Through some research I've discovered that approximately 95% of all people are naturally immune from leprosy. And it's now treatable. And your limbs do not fall off. With only a couple of weeks of treatment leprosy is no longer communicable. That doesn't mean that the people you'll encounter here have been treated, but it's comforting to know that only 5% of our visitors are susceptible to the disease and less than one out of a thousand (by our experience) are infected with it. It would take away the sense of adventure and danger if we knew in advance who were susceptible to the disease, or if we scouted out neighborhoods to discover who are infected before visiting the houses. Be prepared to love them all – lepers with

tuberculosis included.

Finally, all of you, live in harmony with one another; be sympathetic, love as brothers, be compassionate and humble. – 1 Peter 3:8

Chapter Ten Discussion Questions

1. Are you willing to touch someone with leprosy? Or tuberculosis?

2. What precautions should you take to keep from being infected by others?

3. Will you carry any hand sanitizer with you?

11

Revolutionary Taxes

The fire-fight was far enough away that we never heard the sounds of the gun fire, but close enough to affect daily life in our neighborhood. The Philippine military encountered a band of rebel soldiers, resulting in three dead and several badly injured. Military checkpoints appeared in odd locations along the highway and soldiers boarded every bus to inspect the passengers. Dogs barked incessantly at night as military patrols coursed through the neighborhoods in search of enemies that never materialized. And, based on intelligence obtained by the army, all the houses in Barangay Uno were searched. Helicopters seemed to be everywhere. It was an uneasy time that ended after a month or so, and life has resumed to 'normal' (if there is such a thing here.)

Several years ago I spotted a group of armed men in the early morning hours near the highway, but they quickly disappeared. I would only be guessing if I said who they were, but none were in uniform and several sported haircuts that were clearly not military. Once in awhile I am advised to avoid certain places because they are 'hot spots' where soldiers and New People's Army (NPA) guerillas are hunting one another. I take heed of such advisements.

There's no question that our province hosts a small population of NPA guerillas. Maybe even a bit larger than small. They have sympathizers and employ intelligence officers, and I have no doubt that they know who we are and what we do. And it is also clear that they have chosen not to bother us. Perhaps they leave us alone because we serve the Lord, but more likely they leave us alone because we also serve the poor. Our constituents are the same as theirs, but we've chosen to overcome poverty and corruption one soul at a time, not through the use of force.

On November 23rd, 2009, fifty-seven people were brutally massacred, including thirty-two media workers, to prevent Esmael Mangudadatu from filing a certificate of candidacy to campaign for the governor's office in Magindinao. Their convoy traveling to file his candidacy paperwork was met by nearly 200-armed men who savagely killed the aspiring candidate's wife, his sister and friends, and every journalist brave enough to accompanying them. Innocent occupants of a vehicle following the convoy were also murdered just for being in the wrong place at the wrong time. Several members of the powerful Ampatuan family have been arrested and, as I write this, are currently awaiting trial. The arrests have not diminished their powerful grip in the territory they control.

Presidential elections were recently held in the Philippines and several regions have been tagged by the Commission on Election as 'hotspots' due to intimidation by private armies. The New People's Army also gets into the action during elections, insisting that every candidate pay for a 'permit' to campaign. Refusal to pay the rebels for a 'permit' or reneging on promised payments results in unspecified punishment, but candidates fear the range of possible forms of retribution and pay to be 'protected.' This year the NPA is expected to net somewhere between three to five BILLION pesos! [2] (That's $65M - $109M, or up to $24,000 for each of the estimated 4500 NPA fighters.) The typical income in my neighborhood is between $3.00 and $4.00 per day, so there's more than political appeal to join forces with the rebels.

Shadow governments exist around the world. Regional warlords with private armies control territories that 'legitimate' governments simply avoid. Around the world there are 'unofficial' organizations that control territories in much the same way that gangs

---

[2] NPA to rake in billions during elections – abscbnNEWS.com
03/08/2010

control certain blocks of turf in large cities. They offer protection to those who cooperate with them and extract payment in return. Duly constituted governments (those recognized by the United Nations) know who they are, where they are and what they do, but are powerless to exert authority over them. Rather than foolishly fight against such organizations, we, as ambassadors of Christ, need to understand what Romans 13:1 says - *there is no authority except that which God has established.* And make no mistake about it – *they have authority.*

I have no reason to believe that our missionaries will encounter any members from a 'shadow' government while visiting Aurora – I never see them and they leave us alone. It's important, however, to understand that not all authority wears name tags or uniforms. Listen to your host missionary should a situation arise that involves 'alternative authority', and follow their advice knowing they have your best interest in mind.

Everyone must submit himself to the governing authorities, for there is no authority except that which God has established. - Romans 13:1

Chapter Eleven Discussion Questions

1. Describe any political instability in the region where you are going.

2. Is your host providing you with any sort of security detail? If so, why?

3. Will you be viewed as either an ally or enemy of the police, military, local or national government?

4. If confronted by any 'alternate authority' from a shadow government, are all the members of your team in agreement regarding your response?

5. Just a word of advice: make sure that all members of the team understand that politics in some cultures can be very dangerous. Avoid all political discussions!

12

K & R Insurance

The Chubb Group of insurance companies offers a new product called "K&R" insurance. The 'K' stands for Kidnap and the "R" is for ransom, which it will pay if you are abducted while traveling internationally. I recently watched the ransom demand, initially set at $7 million, drop to $3 million for Britons Paul and Rachel Chandler. They were sailing around-the-world until they were captured in October 2009 by Somali pirates who boarded their yacht off the Seychelles. Celebrities and the wealthy are most at risk when it comes to kidnap for ransom, but missionaries and aid volunteers have also become targets when traveling into regions where such events are common.

Kidnap for ransom is quite unlikely when visiting our region of the Philippines, but I would suggest you investigate K&R insurance if you plan to travel to certain islands in the Mindanao region. Missionaries have no immunity from bandits (and other bad guys.) But there are common sense things we can do to minimize our exposure to those who prey on others. We don't announce our travel plans in advance – even within our church. It prevents our bus from being intercepted in the mountains by men with evil hearts. Do I expect such things to happen if we announced details of our travel plans? No. But there's no reason to offer an opportunity for thieves, bandits, kidnappers, and others who might plan evil to victimize innocent travelers. Our arrival and departure plans, mode of transportation, lodging arrangements, etc … should be provided to others only on a need-to-know basis. Keeping our details and itinerary requires minimal sharing. It's just a precaution.

When I was in Hong Kong I read an article in the *South China Morning Post* about a visiting couple who jumped into a taxi at the airport, and rather than end up at their hotel, were found naked in a remote area in the New Territories. Everything they brought with them, including their clothes and passports, had been stolen. It happens all the time. If a driver seems too eager to get you into their taxi or van, avoid them. Let your host make your travel arrangements for you.

Commercial buses are generally considered a safe mode of transportation in the Philippines, but occasionally I hear about an armed robbery on a provincial bus leaving Manila. Bandits here rarely, if ever, act alone. If in such a situation, cooperation is critical. Assume that at least two other bandits are blending in with other passengers waiting to deal with anyone who refuses to cooperate.

I've traveled thousands of miles on commercial transportation in the Philippines without incident and yet remain alert to all possibilities when on commercial busses, jeepneys or taxis. Typically we charter our own transportation, but it's really more of a convenience issue than a safety concern.   With our own driver we can stop to eat wherever we desire, pull over to rest if someone becomes sick, or stop at the mall to shop for needed items and exchange our dollars into pesos.

In the Philippines it's common to see groups of men gathered to drink gin and/or beer at night. They rarely go home until they've run out of money or a fight has broken out. For this reason I discourage travel at night, and prefer our missionaries to remain together at our lodging after dark. Even meek men become bold and aggressive when intoxicated, and diplomacy may not be an option – it's simply better to avoid such situations than to regret the outcome of an ugly encounter with drunks.

In many places around the world a visitor will be viewed as an oddity and people will gawk at you as you pass by. It's no different here in the Philippines; sometimes you are met with smiles, and other times with hard stares that make you feel uncomfortable. But make no mistake about it – you have many eyes watching you. For criminals who salivate over the prospect of finding a foreigner alone, they are watching you more carefully than others. In summary:

everything you do or say is being scrutinized and evaluated. Don't

compromise your safety by sharing too much information or stepping

outside of the security rules set by your team or advised by your host.

The LORD is my strength and my shield; my heart trusts in him, and I am helped. My heart leaps for joy and I will give thanks to him in song. Psalm 28:1

Chapter Twelve Discussion Questions

1. Have you requested that your host missionary avoid announcing your travel and lodging plans?

2. How can your team minimize exposure to bandits and thieves?

3. Will your team be traveling in public transportation or will you contract private transportation?

4. What, if any, activities are scheduled for your team after dark?

5. Does your team have a partner policy, preventing team members from ever being alone?

13 Ugly Visitors

As we prepared for our mission trip, Stan complained to me about the team covenant that we wanted him to sign. He was a heavy smoker and felt that our total abstinence policy from tobacco products while on mission was an extreme position. He reluctantly signed the covenant, but had absolutely no intention of living without cigarettes for two weeks. When we first arrived in the Philippines he hid in his room or stayed inside of a restroom to smoke, but after a couple of days he opted to smoke openly. Stan chose defiance over self-sacrifice, and soon decided that none of the rules in the covenant applied. Before the end of the first week he found a place to drink the cold beer he'd been craving. And before the end of the trip he demonstrated contempt for any teammate who dared challenge his behavior. Stan became a hindrance to our efforts to put Christ on display. Stan should never have been permitted to be part of the mission team. He didn't serve the church in any capacity while home, so why did we think that he would serve the Lord on foreign soil?

It is a disservice to those who are truly called to serve, an embarrassment to the sending church, and a frustration to the foreign host when self-centered, 'nominal' Christians are permitted to participate in missions. Please don't get me wrong. I am not their judge, nor am I suggesting that they are any less of a believer than I am; I'm simply a sinner who has accepted God's grace. What I'm saying is that we need to have a vetting process in place for those who wish to serve on foreign soil. Some people are simply too self-absorbed to sacrifice creature comforts without complaining to the point of exasperating teammates. Others are unable to accept that there are other (and sometimes better) ways of doing things than 'the way that we do it back home'. Some come as willing, but empty vessels, without even a basic understanding of their own spiritual gifts. Some come because the waterfall or beach photos enticed them. Team leaders must be bold enough to explain that international missions begin with a calling, require equipping, and demand selflessness. Unless all three conditions are met, the result can prove to be a detriment to the host missionary.

Bert is a talented construction worker in his mid-fifties. His local church association sponsored a mission trip to the Philippines specifically to help build our church. Bert's pastor encouraged him to participate because Bert knew every aspect of construction. He is an expert brick mason, a carpenter, an electrician and a plumber. He is also a chronic whiner who expects that everything be catered to his whims. He was bold enough to demand that we send someone to Manila (eight hours away by bus) to buy a bag of grits for him to eat, which my wife did for him! He refused to eat his breakfast unless grits were included. He smoked like a D-Liner bus (even though he signed a team covenant agreeing to refrain from smoking during the trip) and Bert cursed like the evil protagonist in an "R" rated Hollywood action film.

Before his ten days in our province was finished he had frustrated his team members to the point of ugly verbal exchanges in front of people he came to assist. Our volunteers bent over backwards to cook Bert fried chicken, fried breaded okra, mashed potatoes with brown gravy, and corn bread (even though we have no oven.) They became thoroughly discouraged by Bert's criticism of every meal placed before him. Bert's foul mouth and angry demeanor repelled the volunteers who worked alongside him. Christ was clearly not on display in his life.

To make matters worse, all of the power tools that Bert carried with him to the Philippines proved to be worthless. They all required 110 volt electricity, and everything here is 220 volt. The local power company failed to connect power to our construction site despite the fact that we submitted a work order more than ninety days in advance. The 10,000-watt generator we brought to the construction site wouldn't pull enough amps to operate the circular saw and it kept shutting off. This infuriated Bert, who threw boards, tools, and frequent vulgarity-laced temper tantrums. Seven years later people still refer to 'Brother Bert' and his anger management issues; he's become a local synonym for undisciplined behavior.

I'm sure that his pastor wasn't shocked when told about Bert's behavior while serving on the mission field. Bert's foul mouth and angry disposition were clearly known, and his cigarette habit was considered no big deal in a county that is known for its tobacco harvest. Do we simply overlook such shortcomings, understanding than none of us have yet arrived at perfection? Or do we choose to minimize the damage that can be caused by a poor attitude like Bert's? Personally, I hope never to see another missionary like Bert. But unfortunately, churches seem either unwilling or unable to weed out people who possess not one single fruit of the spirit from participating in missions. People with glaring shortcomings, such as Bert, don't properly represent Christ, and shouldn't be brought halfway around the world to become an embarrassment to their host or to the cause of Christ.

Let me provide you with another example. Ruth is a young woman who has come to the Philippines several times. She loves it here and would live here permanently if she could raise the support.

The only problem is that she comes here to be served and not to serve. Although she's been here multiple times, she has yet to perform any form of ministry or participate in planned activities. Those who contributed funds to support her mission trips have been ripped off and deserve a refund. Ruth has befriended several Filipinos who cater to her every whim and she soaks it up. I witnessed one of our pastor's wives spoon feed Ruth her entire meal! And while Ruth was being spoon-fed each bite of her meal I observed an elderly couple on the team clearing dishes from the table and washing them. The contrast between them was clear; some came to serve, but Ruth came to be served. People love Ruth and so do I. But I think most people would admit that she is emotionally immature, easily irked, pouts, and is lazy. So let me be honest about her contribution to the mission. In my estimate Ruth has been a net negative.

When I organized our first trip to the Philippines, our church had no established eligibility policy for those who wanted to participate. Personally, I was eager to recruit anyone willing to come along and excited when anyone attended our planning meetings. I was naïve and eagerly welcomed everyone to participate. My heart has been changed by several very difficult personalities who not only failed to minister to the people of the Philippines, but made it difficult for their team members to remain focused. One was a single, middle-aged man who refused to keep his hands off of all the young girls. He was advised that his hugs were alien to the local culture and that his insistence on holding their hands or placing his arms around the teenage girls was simply inappropriate. He refused to listen, but because I couldn't tell him "no" he was permitted to return to the Philippines a second time to repeat his behavior all over again.

Martha is a godly woman whom I greatly admire. She's been to the Philippines several times and is passionate about the ministry here. Her adult son, in his mid-thirties, expressed an interest in participating with our next mission team, and Martha was exuberant about the thought of serving on a mission trip with her son. Martha's son was a Christian, but had fallen away from the Lord and the church about three years before in the midst of an ugly divorce. I told her that he would be welcome to come along, but not on the next trip. I suggested that she bring him to church and allow us to know him first and discover his heart. As much as Martha wanted her son to return to the Lord, the mission field is not that place. Missions should be reserved for those who are already committed, who have a contagious faith, in fact, and are willing to share it. Martha was somewhat disappointed, but understood the reasons that we didn't welcome her son as one of our missionaries. Martha continues to return to the Philippines frequently, and I continue to pray for her son and his commitment to the Lord.

Short term missionaries return to their home church carrying great enthusiasm about their experiences. Many people have been used by God in a new or very special way. They may have sensed the closeness of God's spirit and felt a powerful anointing during the trip. Worship they experienced may have been different and powerful. When short-term missionaries return home they are ignited about what they've experienced and want to share their heart with everyone. Because of this, some believe that the mission field is where you send people for them to gain a new passion for the Lord. That it's the place to send your church youth to get them fired up for the Lord. And I've seen it work. But, in honesty, I've seen the negative side of bringing lukewarm believers to the mission field too, and it isn't pretty. We're all irritated when there's no electricity, but we understand that whining won't bring it back. We would all prefer hot running water for our showers, but don't complain about the lack of it every time we bathe. Immature believers tend to place themselves first, and their selfishness drags the entire team down.

Let me specifically address youth pastors on this issue. I know that you want to ignite your youth for Jesus, and that a powerful experience on the mission field has the potential to make a huge impact on your youth. Please be considerate of the others on the team when selecting (yes, *selecting*) potential missionaries. Don't bring along the misfits or troublemakers with the hope that they will be transformed. Yes, it can happen. But you need to set the standard. Don't bring your youth on a mission trip because they (or their parents) think it would be a good idea. Bring those who are growing spiritually and who would benefit the mission. 'Nuf said.

Now let me tell you a horror story that a missionary friend related to me; it provides a perfect example of why you must qualify those who travel with your team as missionaries. Woody, an elderly man nearing retirement, attended a small church in rural Virginia that had no mission activity. When he discovered that his brother's church was going on a trip to Ecuador, Woody asked to go with them. Without knowing anything about Woody, the church welcomed him to the team. During the mission trip Woody became infatuated with an Ecuadoran woman, and he spent most of his time flirting with her. In fact, he proposed marriage to the woman before the team returned home to Virginia. Within two weeks Woody returned to Ecuador to marry his new love. But within days of his return to Ecuador, Woody got into a fierce quarrel with his new fiancée, a church member of the ministry visited by his brother's church. Woody is not a quitter and was determined to find a wife, so he shifted his attention to other women. In his desperate search for a wife he even sent a love letter to the pastor's teenage daughter! The local pastor calls Woody a 'human wrecking ball.' He's divided the church and has caused dissention. Woody may have found what he returned for – a wife, but he's caused nothing but grief for the ministry. He now gets into frequent public fights with his young wife. He's had several encounters with local law enforcement due to his uncontrollable fits of rage. Even local contractors now refuse to work for him because he's cheated several of them.

Woody has done more to discredit the ministry in Ecuador than any one person, to the delight of scoffers and enemies of the cross. The local missionary has asked us to pray that Woody will return to the US with his new family and spare them any further dismay and embarrassment. He says 'we knew that there's an enemy, but we never expected that he would attack through one of our missionaries.'

This chapter has been difficult for me to write because it focuses on an issue that is both negative and difficult to address. But the reality is this: there are people in your church who are not qualified to be sent out as missionaries. If you have no policy regarding missionaries, establish one before you announce plans for a trip. Don't let a person's ability to raise financial support be the determining factor for their suitability for missions. Be willing to ask potential missionaries some tough questions. We don't want to hurt anyone's feelings, but it's far better to restrict participation in missions than to damage a growing ministry halfway around the world by bringing a team comprised of Stan, Bert, Ruth and Woody.

You'll find few who are as passionate about missions as I am. The last thing I want to do is discourage anyone from participation in missions. There are, however, people who should participate by sending others until the Lord prepares them to go.

As dead flies give perfume a bad smell, so a little folly outweighs wisdom and honor. Ecclesiastes 10:1

Chapter Thirteen Discussion Questions

For team leaders:

1. Are there any members on your team who come from outside your church?
2. Did any member of your team argue against items in the team covenant?
3. Have you established a vetting process, or can anyone sign up and join your mission team?
4. Are there any team members that are 'invisible' (not serving in any capacity) within your church?
5. What sort of interview process is in place for prospective team members?
6. Are there any unaccompanied minors? (If so, obtain notarized permission.)
7. Are all prospective team members medically cleared for the trip?
8. Do any of the prospective team members have a history of emotional instability or diagnosed mental illness?
9. Have you requested and performed criminal background investigations?

For team members:

1. Do you have any personal vices/habits that you'll have difficulty with on the trip?
2. Do you view participation in missions as a right or as a privilege?
3. Are you willing to set aside your desires and comforts for the sake of the mission?

14   It's Just a Rash

If you arrive in Manila from the east coast of the United States you are upside down – literally halfway around the world. You're twelve time zones away from home (unless it is daylight savings time), which is as far away as you can get. Your day is now night and your night is now day. Your sleep schedule is messed up, and your immune system is weakened in the process. It's horribly frustrating to travel this far and end up sick in bed, unable to participate in the mission for that which you came and called.

Let's face it, there are some illnesses that, no matter how hard you try to avoid them, attack you and render you helpless. You can't avoid breathing the recycled air on the long international flight. Spreading germs amongst the team members is inevitable. You will be living in close community, shaking hands with many strangers, and will be exposed to some potent new viruses eager to meet you. Your bathing water will likely be bacterial soup. There are, however, some basic things you need to consider in order to remain healthy while on mission.

First, and most importantly, arrive fit. Get in shape before you travel. It will help your body deal with the lack of sleep, change in diet, and rigors you're unaccustomed to. Commit yourself to a daily workout for ninety days prior to your departure. Start slowly, but make sure that you can walk several miles each day by the time you get on the plane. Those who are seriously out of shape, morbidly obese, or unhealthy may not deal well with jungle heat, long walks, or long periods of standing. In the afternoon heat I witnessed one of our visitor's cheeks turn noticeably pink; within minutes her face and neck became bright red. Her disposition changed as her discomfort increased and her heavy sweat stopped flowing. She went outside to sit in the shade, hoping for a breeze because the electricity was out. Soon she was lying down, with people fanning her and racing to find a glass of potable water for her to drink. The heat here quickly overpowers those who are in poor physical health. Don't be the team member who requires extra care, misses activities, and causes worry because of poor physical conditioning.

A highly contagious leper attends our church in the Philippines each week. He takes no medicine to treat the condition even though it can be obtained free through the Philippine government (thanks to the World Health Organization.) Despite his leprosy, he greets others with handshakes and pats us all on the back, knowing, but not caring that he's carrying and transmitting bacteria capable of crippling and killing. This evening our pastor is visiting our local government officials to discuss a plan of action. We've agreed to provide his family with food (the leper, not our pastor) while he undergoes treatment, and we're waiting for a reply. Fortunately 95% of the population is naturally immune against leprosy. You can pray that you are not one of the 5% who is susceptible to this terrible (but treatable) disease, but you need to know that there are people you'll encounter on the mission field who are infected with serious and transmissible diseases.

Tuberculosis is the best example of such a disease. As I examined this disease I encountered articles on several websites that declared as much as one third of the world's population may be infected with some variety of tuberculosis. The percentage of the world's population infected is reportedly falling. But the actual number of infection continues to increase as the world's population increases. A respected pediatrician in our provincial capital told me that nearly 90% of the people in our region have been exposed to tuberculosis. They are not all infected, yet they test positive when a TB skin test is administered. Chest X-rays are needed to determine if they actually have an active case of the disease (which kills more than fifty percent of its victims if left untreated.)

We've never sent a visitor home with either tuberculosis or leprosy, so don't consider backing out of the greatest adventure you may ever experience because of a remote infection possibility. It's possible that you can be hit by an asteroid, a falling coconut, or lightning, but you wouldn't be dissuaded by such remote possibilities. And there are precautions we can take against disease.

Carry hand sanitizer in with you in your backpack and use it. Don't sanitize immediately after shaking hands with someone – it's insensitive, suggesting to them that you think they are somehow dirty enough to contaminate you. Follow the same advice we hear every flu season: wash your hands frequently, cough into your sleeve or a tissue and not your hands, eat immune boosting foods (such as citrus, red chili peppers, garlic, carrots, and fish.) Get proper rest, hydrate yourself with plenty of water, avoid touching your eyes, nose and mouth, and get exercise.

The Center for Disease Control and Prevention provides detailed health instructions for people traveling anywhere on planet earth. Take a look at their website to obtain country-specific health advice: http://wwwnc.cdc.gov/travel/destinations/list.aspx

I won't go into detail about which immunizations for you to get because this site provides all the details you need. It provides common sense methods of preventing disease. We're told to apply insect repellant with Deet to avoid insects. We can also protect ourselves by wearing long pants, a long sleeved shirt, and a hat. The CDC suggests staying indoors during the peak mosquito hours of dusk and dawn. Except for the long sleeved shirt, I do these things.

Since I mentioned insects, I need to inform you that there are bugs here that you've never seen before, such as flying, biting cockroaches. It is not just possible, but highly likely that ants will get into any food you stash away, even if it is in your backpack in a Ziploc bag!

A small fuzzy caterpillar fell on my son, Dylan, from a tree we were using for shade during a local elementary school visit. His ear and neck broke out with blood-red blisters and huge welts in a matter of seconds. Moments later his shoulder and the back of his arm swelled up and the itching began to burn. The itch was too intense for him to resist scratching it. It spread quickly to his hands and face. Our Filipino friends squeezed the juice from a calamansi (small lime-like citrus fruit) onto his welts and the itching stopped. The rash remained for days from a momentary encounter with this caterpillar. Avoid contact with any unfamiliar creature, even fuzzy little caterpillars!

A young boy, just ten years old named Jerold is in the local clinic as I write this, suffering from what appears to be rabies. He was bitten by a dog that later died, which is an ominous sign. His mother suffers from mental problems and is unable to provide him with proper supervision. His grandmother is poor and waited too long to seek treatment. We know these things about the family because they live here in my neighborhood. Jerold is now salivating uncontrollably, has a frozen jaw, is unable to speak, and is in terrible pain. His eyes dart around the room and sparks of consciousness appear in them only every few seconds. He has an unquenchable thirst and drinks whatever is provided to him. I cried when I visited him and his grandmother at the clinic, knowing that only a handful of people have ever survived rabies once symptoms appear.[3] Rabies is specifically addressed in the chapter called "Critters", but is also a medical condition here that you obviously don't want to experience.

Sharon began to freak out when large red stripes started appearing on both legs. After an hour and two Benadryl® capsules the stripes vanished. I witnessed the welts on her legs and understand why she panicked. It was her first experience with grass allergy, but this honestly looked like much more than an allergy. Bright red stripes, more than a foot long, were all over her legs and it

[3] Jerold's case of rabies turned out to be tetanus and he is now fully recovered!

looked awful. We were preparing to go to the doctor's office when a girl from our church explained that it was a grass allergy, one that she also suffers from. I'm pretty sure that they used some Vicks Vaporub® as the cure.

It's not just medical issues to be concerned about, but dental conditions as well. Devon developed a toothache before we left the province to return to Manila. By the time we arrived at our hotel his face was swollen and he was in severe pain. He required painkillers and antibiotics, but smartly opted to have his dental work performed back in the United States. Another visitor, Francis, developed a nasty abscessed tooth that eventually required extraction. Make sure your 'choppers' are prepared for the trip too.

Travis is a doctor who has been to the Philippines twice. He picked up a bad stomach 'bug' the first time (blaming it on buko juice from the young coconuts, but I'm skeptical.) The second trip he encountered the worst headaches he'd ever had and believes he was attacked by meningitis. Travis is young, energetic and in good health. Even though you're physically fit, there's no guarantee that you'll remain healthy throughout the trip. Isolate yourself from the others if it all possible when you have something that you believe is communicable.

I woke up four days ago with my eyes welded shut. I had to wash them to remove the ooze and mucus. They were blood red and burned; and four days later they still itch and burn. 'Pink eye' or conjunctivitis, locally known as 'sore' eye has attacked my entire family and we're all suffering. This monster of a virus (or bacteria, depending upon the variety) could easily bring a short-term mission trip to a halt. This is an affliction that is very easily transmitted, so even if one member of the team comes in contact with it, others are soon to share it. We wouldn't want to share both the Gospel and 'sore eye', so our outreach efforts would be suspended for anyone impacted with this affliction. Airlines won't permit you to board an aircraft while you are carrying anything so highly contagious, which adds inconvenience and expense to mission impact. As believers, submitted to 'all authority' we wouldn't try to hide our affliction with sunglasses and travel anyway. First, hiding an ailment is wrong, but more pragmatically because US Customs and Immigration will make you remove your sunglasses and will quarantine you at your port of arrival as you try to sneak back into the US. Your co-passengers, ticket agents, security screeners, and those who greet you when you return will appreciate you more if you change your flight plans and heal completely before you return home.

There are so many things to talk about when I think of insects: ants, bees, flying (and biting) cockroaches, however, perhaps the nastiest things you'll encounter here are far smaller than insects. Microbes are microscopic organisms that transmit diseases. You can ingest them, inhale them, absorb them through your skin, or even by touching your eyes once you've been exposed. The most common exposure comes through food and beverages. Avoid eating food from street vendors. Never drink beverages with ice in them (the water to make the ice must be presumed to be contaminated.) Don't share drinking glasses (very commonly done here in the Philippines.) Drink only bottled or purified water. Remain alert to potential microbial invasion and you'll likely avoid this problem.

Don't hesitate to seek medical attention if you believe that there's something seriously wrong with you. The local cure (such as calimansi juice on the blisters) may be worth trying, but don't allow yourself to be 'sidelined' unnecessarily while waiting for folk cures to work. Follow the health guidelines established for your team. And listen carefully to any supplemental cautions provided by your host missionary.

They loathed all food and drew near the gates of death. - Psalm 107:18

Chapter Fourteen Discussion Questions

1. Are you physically fit for the trip?

2. Name five things you can do to avoid flu contamination. (It applies to other bacteria and viruses as well.)

3. Which inoculations are recommended for the region you're going to? Have you obtained them?

4. Do you plan to bring along some heavy-duty insect repellant?

5. Would sunblock be advisable for you to consider?

6. Are you allergic to anything? If so does your team leader know? Will you bring allergy medication with you?

7. Do you need any dental work that should be completed prior to departure?

8. Where will your team obtain drinking water?

9. Are there any medications that you need to bring along? Will your prescription last the entire trip?

15 Pulling Teeth

A flurry of news stories reported that the 2007 Heisman Trophy winner, Tim Tebow, performed circumcisions on young boys while on a mission trip in the southern Philippines. Criticism from the online community was fierce, noting that Mr. Tebow has no medical training and was unqualified to "operate on some poor kid's junk." Hundred of comments were posted, most too crude to for me to print, mocking missionaries who 'think that they are gods'. But many also brought up a good point: there are rules that need to be followed even in third world nations. But, in defense of Tim Tebow, circumcisions here are not generally performed by physicians. He knows this as he was born in and raised by missionary parents here in the Philippines. Circumcision is a tradition here, a rite of passage, for boys at the age of thirteen. Our local circumcision '*specialist*' is a gay school teacher who gleefully performs the operations in the water of the Malupa River.

So let's examine some medical mission trip issues. Each state in the U.S. has a medical licensing requirement, and your ability to practice medicine is confined within the borders of the state in which you are licensed. Without special permissions or permits, it's against the law to practice medicine where you're not licensed. The same applies to other nations; even third world nations have rules that must be followed when it comes to practicing medicine.

In September 2010, six church workers were arrested in Zimbabwe for operating without proper medical licenses. They had been working in Zimbabwe for more than a decade without ever being questioned, so they were understandably shocked when their workers were jailed. Their ministry, helping AIDS orphans, is important and commendable work. But allow me be brutally honest about this subject; it's our own fault if our missionary team members end up in foreign jails because they lacked the necessary credentials. Ignorance is no excuse – we must ask what is required, especially if we are providing medical treatment.

The Philippines requires visiting physicians to secure a "Special Temporary Permit" for non-local physicians who intend to perform medicine in the Philippines. It requires a letter from the local sponsoring association addressed to the Secretary of the Commission or Chairman of the Professional Regulatory Board. Team members need to photocopy license information and submit everything required at least ninety days before a medical team travels to the Philippines.

There are also special requirements for medications that are being imported to the Philippines with the team. A locally licensed physician must meet any medicine shipments at the airport. And a locally licensed physician must participate (supervise) the team at all times while they are performing medical procedures. Are these requirements strictly enforced? No. We hosted three medical teams here before we even knew that such requirements existed. But keep in mind that many of the same requirements apply to dentists, optometrists, and veterinarians. Professions which require licensing in the US likely require licenses in other nations as well.

We hired a local dentist to extract teeth for three days. That's all he did, pull teeth for six hours each day. Each extraction took only a couple of minutes, but the line of people awaiting extractions grew longer and longer. There were very old people, preschool-aged children and students skipping school to have their problem teeth pulled for free. Keep in mind that this was *done entirely without anesthesia*! When things started getting busy the dentist asked for me to help him pull teeth. By this he clearly meant that he wanted for me to set up another chair, use his tools to reach into people's mouths and yank their teeth out! He said that it would be permissible as long as I was under his direct supervision. Although I would love to place 'dentist' on my missionary resume, I've decided that some things are best left to professionals.

Pharmaceutical companies or drug stores in many countries don't appreciate strangers from another nation, another faith, giving away for free what they sell for a living. The free medicine is a blessing to those who receive them, but some may view you as a direct challenge to their livelihood. This also includes vitamins. For reasons I don't understand, vitamins are very expensive here in the Philippines. Because they are pricey and highly profitable those who sell vitamins don't appreciate foreigners giving away prenatal vitamins, children's vitamins, 50 plus vitamins, men's vitamins, or women's vitamins. Here in the Philippines angry vendors may quietly curse you, but they are unlikely to harm you or interfere with your mission efforts. In other places (such as Zimbabwe with AIDS drugs) you may find that these people have powerful friends who can shut your operation down and cause you enormous grief.

A mix of experienced and novice carpenters, masons, electricians and plumbers from your church may combine their talents to build a church, a restroom at a school, a home for a widow, or a day care center in a foreign community. It's one of the most common activities performed on mission trips. But even if your host missionary tells you that blueprints, building permits and that entire bureaucracy are unnecessary, please go through the entire legal process anyway. We built classrooms here in the Philippines for a pre-school, skipping the 'bureaucracy' of needless blueprints and permits. Why should we have added anything extra or unnecessary to our effort? But obtaining a license to open the preschool proved to be a challenge without 'certified' blueprints and an approved building permit for the buildings. The opening of the school was delayed by months for paperwork that cost us less than $100.

In some locations (not the Philippines) you may also offend local labor unions that require a percentage of the jobs on any construction site. You don't want such confrontation when representing Christ. Union confrontations are generally not pleasant.

Here in the Philippines, the architect who designs a building is held liable for any injuries, deaths or property damage if the building collapses in an earthquake or storm. In the absence of a culpable architect, your local missionary or pastor may be facing charges should a structure collapse. Don't take short cuts in this area. The required permits may require time, but are generally not expensive. Plan to have these requirements completed *before* your team arrives in country.

And since we're examining legalities, understand this: even during time of calamity, we need to follow established protocol and observe all legal requirements. On January 12th, 2010, more than 212,000 people were killed in Haiti from a massive earthquake. Aid from around the world poured into Haiti as quickly as possible. Churches quickly gathered money and materials to send to Haiti, and volunteer missionaries responded to the crises as quickly as they could. People in Haiti were injured, orphaned, hungry and without shelter, without clean drinking water or hope. It was a humanitarian crisis impossible to ignore, and being so close to the US, the response from American churches was enormous.

Less than a month after the earthquake, in the midst of chaos and desperation, ten American missionaries were arrested attempting to bring thirty three children from the earthquake-stricken region into the Dominican Republic. They were charged with kidnapping – a charge for which there is no bail and which could result in a life sentence. Now I don't know about you, but I'd be a bit miffed if my team leader made a decision that placed me in a Haitian prison for the rest of my life.

The Idaho-based missionaries who were arrested in Haiti endured quite an ordeal. They were denied bail and were pelted with stones by Haitians who despised the 'preferential treatment' they were given in captivity. They became the vortex of a storm of international intrigue, but the Lord delivered them through the ordeal. All of the kidnapping charges brought against them were dropped, though one of the missionaries still faces the strange charge of "organization of irregular trips".

In the chapter entitled "Collide with Nothing" I explained the driving conditions here in the Philippines. Let me reiterate: you don't want to drive here. If you have an accident you could be placed on 'International Hold' and remain here until any charges or litigation against you have been resolved. The insurance you have on your vehicles back in the US will not cover you here. And even though the Philippines will honor your US driver's license for a period of time after your arrival in the Philippines, you should leave the driving here to Filipinos. Driving here places you and your team at unnecessary risk.

Many times I've used the old adage, "It's easier to get forgiveness than permission" when I am faced with what seems to be insurmountable obstacles. I'm suggesting that you do otherwise. You don't want your mission trip to flounder after all of the prayer, spiritual preparation, and expense because of some simple paperwork glitch.

Let me offer yet another example. A 14- year-old girl came with our team to the Philippines several years ago. As we were on the long flight from Detroit to Nagoya I began to wonder if we could get her into the country without a legal guardian. Or back into the US!

Why did that never cross my mind during our planning meetings? Luckily she looked much older than fourteen and was able to pass through immigration and customs with the rest of us. But I did go back and research the requirement. To my horror I discovered that anyone fifteen years of age or younger requires a parent, legal guardian, or signed and notarized permission for another person to escort them internationally. Immediately I designed such a permission slip, and made sure that it was filled out the next time we had a young team member. Without it, Henry would never have been permitted into the Philippines. He was thirteen, but looked younger, and we were asked to produce his 'guardianship' papers at the immigration counter. Fortunately we had them. But we discovered something else we hadn't anticipated: there was a special processing fee for unaccompanied minors, and the process to pay it took over an hour at the airport and added $100 to our team expense.

As missionaries we can pull teeth, circumcise young boys, and build whatever we wish without the need for legalities or paperwork. We can get away with riding atop vehicles and hanging off the sides of them. We can smuggle items through customs so that they're not taxed or confiscated. But as Christ followers, let's be excellent in all that we do, providing no reason for others to attack us. In your planning process, ask yourself, "is there any special permit, tax, or license might be required?" There's time before each trip to make

sure that we 'render unto Caesar' those things that Caesar is due.

Everything is permissible", - but not everything is beneficial. 1 Cor 10:23

Chapter Fifteen Discussion Questions

1. Will any of your planned mission activities require special licensing or local certification? (Medical or dental in particular.)

2. Will any of your planned activities require special permits? (Construction projects)

3. Are there items, such as blueprints, that need approval before you arrive?

4. Will any planned activity offend local unions? If so, how will you address the issue?

5. Do you need to obtain permission to bring along any team members (minors)?

6. Are there any special taxes required for items that you are bringing with you?

16 Where's Mama?

Prepare to meet some interesting characters and to be heartbroken when you visit house-to-house here. You'll find babies left in charge of yet smaller babies. You'll discover severely disfigured people who are unable to communicate, yet remain at home alone. You'll encounter blind children who remain at home without any hope for an education or an occupation. On one visit you may meet an elderly couple who hunger for your companionship and beg you not to leave. And in the next house you might stumble into a den of drug dealers who become upset that you've seen too much and angrily insist that you need to leave the neighborhood. No, *the country*, you need to get out of the country! And you'll find drunks, lots of them. They cluster in groups here and can be found at any time of the day. This chapter is designed to prepare you for situations you'll encounter as you spend time in the neighborhoods.

It was shocking, even to me, when we found them alone in the house. The small boy, perhaps three years old wore only a T-shirt and a smile. His baby sister, just old enough to walk, was naked and frightened. Both looked unkempt and were dirty, and Barbara didn't want to leave them alone. It was both mother instinct and our cultural

expectation to protect kids of this age. We waited about ten minutes

for the mother, or anyone for that matter, to materialize, but it didn't

happen. Our translator walked to the closest house to find out who

was watching the kids and returned to tell us that the father had

recently abandoned the family and that the mother was out looking for

food. The neighbor seemed unconcerned that the kids were alone,

and our two Filipino escorts weren't particularly concerned by the

situation either. We bought some crackers at the nearest sari-sari

store and left the kids with some crackers to eat and continued

through the rest of the barrio.

Rarely do you notice people missing arms, legs, or eyes in the

United States because they're normally fitted with artificial limbs or

glass eyes. But here, and in most of the developing world, you see

many who are missing limbs; some as the result of accidents, but

many as a result of birth defects. And you may find yourself in an

uncomfortable position, deciding whether to look at the massive tumor

on someone's face or try to ignore it. You'll see grossly disfigured

faces, goiters the size of another head, children missing fingers, and

you'll come face-to-face with some very frightening medical

conditions.

I encountered a young man who had taken his grandmother from her home to the community shelter as the rain continued to fall and some of the homes began to flood. His grandmother was nearly dead and smelled like urine. Her eyes were dull and lifeless and she was motionless, yet we made sure that she heard the Gospel. She responded when we asked for a response, but we have no idea why she responded. Her movement at that time could have been mere coincidence, but my conscious is clear. I don't skip anyone as we roam through neighborhoods – I consider each and every encounter as a 'divine appointment'. That includes the rowdy, shirtless guys standing along the roadside smoking cigarettes. That also includes construction workers mixing cement. It also includes merchants in the neighborhood sari-sari stores. When it comes to the Gospel, nobody should be skipped. It would be a shame to travel halfway around the world for a divine appointment that you walked right past.

In many of the houses you'll see the true depth of poverty that permeates the lives of two billion people on our planet. I recently went to a house that contained only a couple of homemade furniture items, a bench seat made from bamboo, and a plywood table with four bamboo chairs. The unpainted plank walls were completely barren except for a laminated high school diploma and a calendar from a local business (featuring a near-naked woman on it.) The woman of the house was in her mid-thirties. She had been cooking and offered us food. We accepted her offer, but had to eat in shifts as she only had three plates, three spoons and one shared drinking glass. Your life may be radically affected by the people you encounter, not because of their personality, but because of the conditions in which they live.

It's okay to be heartbroken when you see people who are hurting, in need, or who are living in hopelessness. Cry with them, be generous towards them, but never forget that what they need most— more than the air they breathe —is to submit to the Lordship of Jesus Christ.

He who is kind to the poor lends to the Lord, and he will reward him for what he has done. - Proverbs 19:17

Chapter Sixteen Discussion Questions

1. What will you do if confronted by an angry drunk?

2. How will you respond when you encounter people who are grossly disfigured?

3. Have you discussed divine appointments in your planning?

4. Are you prepared to be heartbroken by overpowering poverty?

5. Are you willing to ask your translators or guides to go where the Lord leads you? (Often they may skip intimidating looking men, a group of construction workers, or the owner of the neighborhood store.)

Something 'Magnanimous'

Only a full time missionary could tell you what you're about to read in this chapter, but they won't. Some will hold their tongue because they don't want to 'bite the hand that feeds them'. They wouldn't risk offending the very people who provide them with personal support and who help their ministry in so many ways. Or, perhaps they're more spiritually mature than I am and restrain their thoughts out of love. But if you really want to assist full time missionaries in a meaningful way please pay attention to these words. If you provide financial assistance when visiting a ministry, don't attach strings and conditions that become a burden to your host missionary.

Suppose a shoe store owner hires a handful of part-time, temporary workers to help inventory all of the shoes in the store and sort them by brand, style and size. But when the helpers showed up for work, instead of helping with the inventory and sorting, they decided to sweep the floors, clean the storefront glass, repaint the walls, and rearrange the display racks. The store owner would have no problem redirecting their efforts – after all, he's paying for their help. But your host missionary is not paying for your help, and is so grateful for your involvement, that he will permit you to 'sweep floors, clean glass, repaint walls and rearrange racks' even though 'inventory and sorting' is what he needs from you.

Allow your host missionary to define the needs of the ministry for you. Don't recruit a construction team from your youth group, and then announce to your host missionary, "We'll arrive on July 3rd with fifteen enthusiastic teenagers to help you build something." In fact, don't arrive with a construction team unless you're also bringing the funds to pay for all of the construction materials! A pastor whom I truly love recently offered to send a construction team from his church to help us build"whatever we need." But their summer mission trip plans were changed after I asked the obvious question, "Will you also be providing the funds for the construction materials?"

Most self-supported missionaries don't focus only on the mission; out of necessity they also manage a non-profit organization that operates on a razor thin budget. And the vast majority of donations to our ministry are given to help with very specific needs. If some kind-hearted donor provides us with sponsorship money to send a child to school, I can't reallocate that student's money to help pay for a construction project. The same goes for money donated specifically to help with people's medical needs; I can't (and wouldn't) use medical funds to construct a building. And if someone provides me with money to install a well and pump to provide water for a family without access, that's how the money will be used. It is not realistic to expect your host missionary to have any 'unallocated' funds to assist with your mission.

Let me help all of the small non-profit mission organizations in saying this: please donate to their general funds without any strings attached. Our ministry lifts the burden of the poor through student sponsorships, medical assistance, job creation, and a variety of community-based projects. Each one of these projects is used as a platform for evangelism. Our goal is to make Christ known by showing his love in practical ways. But our biggest need as an organization is not another child sponsorship. We currently have more than 350 students sponsored to school in a geographic area that spans over 250 square miles. This requires an enormous effort to arrange for their shoes, uniforms, school supplies and tuition. Our volunteers often have to make several trips to deliver supplies to the sponsored child if he/she is absent from school or not at home when the team arrives for delivery. Our greater need is gasoline money and the ability to compensate our volunteers for an ever increasing slice of their time.

We recently hosted a short term missionary who arrived with more than $2000 provided by his church to help with the ministry here. He asked me where we needed help, and I told him that the church in San Leonardo needed a cement floor, walls and additional chairs. He said he'd "pray about it," then returned to me the next day to let me know that the Lord had other plans for the money. I then told him that we send out three teams each week who are planting churches in the communities of Bacong, Calao and Zarah, and that we needed money to send them and grow those outreach locations into churches. Once again, he requested a day or two to pray about it and returned and asked me, "What else do you have?" I offered at least four other suggestions, all of which were deemed unacceptable. He returned home with the money and later sent me an e-mail asking for other suggestions. I responded by restating our need to help plant churches and, almost a year later, have heard nothing back from him.

Please let go of any money you give. By this I mean don't attach strings to a donation, insisting that the recipient do something special for you as a result of the donation. Trust your host missionary to use your gift in a way that it is most needed. We received a fifteen dollar donation from one of our missionaries that was given in the name of a child who had passed away in the donor's church. Our missionary said that he wanted "something magnanimous" done with the fifteen dollars. Not only did it need to be 'magnanimous', he requested that we coordinate with him before we spent the money so that he could determine whether our plan for the money was grand enough. After five or six suggestions were rejected over a six month span of time, we offered to provide a small, drivable wooden car (that we purchased for around $25) to a child in a needy family. "Well, maybe if the child was sick or terminally ill …" We settled on the wooden car, but the man insisted that our "obligation"wouldn't be fulfilled until we sent him both photos and video of the recipient child on the car. I will refuse any future *magnanimous* donations.

Please try to work within the framework of the ministry that you visit. Let me provide you with an example. A soft-hearted missionary who comes here frequently can't bear to see children who aren't enrolled in school. Every time she sees a school-aged child who isn't attending school she 'adopts' them, and pays to sponsor them for the school year. This creates a couple of problems. First, the child is not an applicant for our sponsorship program and we need to process all of the application paperwork and obtain photographs. Our local pastors determine applicant eligibility in each community based on a variety of factors, so these students enter the program through a 'back door'. But the more important reason is that children who fail to attend classes (for whatever reason) are far less likely to complete the school year than children whose parents sacrifice food to get them educated. Our missionary friend discovered this when she returned to the Philippines, bringing gifts to each of her sponsored students, only to discover that virtually every one of the 'back door' students had dropped out. Trust the processes your host missionary has established – there are reasons they do what they do.

Be careful not to drag your host missionary into areas that are 'out of scope' for their ministry. For instance, if they don't operate an orphanage, don't bring them an orphan to care for. If they are not trained in the adoption rules for the nation, don't involve them in your effort to adopt a child that you fell in love with on your mission trip. If they don't have a radio or television ministry, don't bring them a donation to start one (unless they've expressed such an interest.) Most missionaries will make every effort to accommodate you in such things. But please understand that they also have only twenty four hours in each day. Every hour they spend to meet your need is one less spent on the mission for which God created them.

Soft-hearted missionaries unwittingly create burdens for their host missionary with what seem to be simple requests, such as: "I want to provide an allowance for my sponsored student; would it be okay if she picks it up daily?" I know the student, and her father is a drunk who would take her allowance from her, so the request seems prudent. She can't bring any money home with her without risking it. But this 'simple' request requires more than one hundred eighty transactions during the school year. Each transaction requires about ten minutes from us. We need to document the transaction in our log book, create a receipt, obtain a signature, and load the transaction into our accounting software. That 'simple' request requires about 1800 minutes, or thirty hours of our time each school year. We would need to hire three full time employees to extend this same courtesy to all 350 of the sponsored elementary, high school and college students. It's not as simple as it seems.

Many of you will find this next statement preposterous: We don't need help with evangelism from short term missionaries – we need help creating disciples! Not many churches in America experience the incredible response to the Gospel that we experience here. Many thousands of people in the Aurora Province have surrendered their lives to Christ during mission trips. Our problem (and what a problem to have!) is that we can't effectively follow up with all who respond to the Gospel. When we lead someone to Christ, but never see them again, it's like having a baby and failing to feed it. My heart breaks for those who remain as infants in Christ because we fail to nourish them. One of the reasons, perhaps, that discipleship is not a priority to short term missionaries is that discipleship is also not a priority in their home church.

We've been through the debate many times: wouldn't it be better to have 5000 'infant' believers who are saved from the flames of Hell than have three hundred maturing disciples? If I knew that Jesus would return tomorrow my answer would be yes. But I believe three hundred true disciples will create more disciples, who will, in turn, create even more disciples. The end result will be far more believers over the years who would also have a greater depth of understanding. Our people would be equipped to preach, teach and share their faith. Our goal is to become more systematic in creating disciples. In fact, the Great Commission says nothing about leading people to an all important decision; Jesus said, "Go, and **make disciples** ..."

In January of each year we host a team that comes to distribute plastic shoe boxes filled with all kinds of goodies. The church loves putting together these boxes that contain soaps, shampoo, pens, pencils, canned meats, candies, and even expensive calculators and wrist watches. They are a true blessing to the poor families who receive them.   The team uses the boxes to share the message of the Gospel, and hundreds of people respond to the message during these trips.

We write down the name of each person who prays to receive Jesus, but, due to lack of workers, are unable to revisit all of these new believers. Then the following January we do it again. I honestly enjoy the evangelism visits, but mourn the fact that we abandon so many new believers to 'spiritual starvation.' Couldn't these

'evangelism' shoe boxes just as easily become 'discipleship'

shoeboxes and be provided to people who attend one of many ten

day discipleship sessions offered? Would fewer people pack them if

they knew that the boxes were not being used for evangelism? I'm

grateful that my home church listens to my concerns, and permits us

to lead the effort here – the shoe boxes provide a platform and are a

tool. How such tools are used should be decided by the host

missionary.

Finally, please make sure to coordinate the dates of your visit

many months in advance. We've had to cancel training classes,

seminars, and skip events that would have strengthened our leaders

in order to accommodate last minute planning. It would be quite

acceptable to ask for me to block off the second half of January to

accommodate your team. It would only be a slight inconvenience if,

once you began pricing airfare, you needed to shift the dates by a day

or two. But shifting dates by weeks or into another month will affect

your host.

As visitors, please respect the wishes of your host missionary.

You'll return home to air conditioning, hot showers and home pizza

delivery after only a week or two. After a few weeks of mind-numbing

TV, your mission trip will become a blurred memory, stirred only by a video or photo of your trip. You'll also share a common experience with others from your church and have a sense of camaraderie with them as a result of your mission experience. But the heavy lifting, the long term work in the nation you visited, still remains in the hands of your host missionary and the local workers.

Plan your trip around the needs of your host missionary. Utilize your funds around those needs as well. Be willing to trust their knowledge of the culture when they suggest things that seem different than the way we might approach a situation. Allow the host missionary to prioritize needs – don't let 'something magnanimous' take the place of something essential.

... so in Christ, we who are many form one body, and each member belongs to all the others. - Romans 12:5

Chapter Seventeen Discussion Questions

1. Is your team's ministry aligned with the needs of your host missionary?

2. Is your team fully funded, relying on no finances from your host missionary?

3. Will your donations have any strings attached? Or is your host missionary free to use your donations towards whatever he views as the ministry's greatest need?

4. Are you willing to ask your host missionary how you can help with existing programs that are set up? (For instance, ask to whom you can sponsor rather than bring him someone that *you* wish to sponsor.)

5. Will you impose obligations on the host missionary when providing money? (Accountability and transparency with the funds are expected. And a request for photos is not unreasonable. But requesting an edited video from them may require more time or skill than they have available. A simple four-minute video takes as long as three hours to upload from the jungle and is frequently interrupted and restarted.)

6. Do you have any plans that may drag your host missionary 'out of scope', creating new activities that he did not suggest?

7. Will you be helping your host missionary create disciples?

Homesick

I have a missionary friend who loves the Quechan people of Peru, and he frequently leads short term missionaries to reach out to people in villages in the region surrounding Cusco. He told me about one young woman (a missionary on his team) who was involved in a relationship with a very jealous boyfriend who required that she"report in" every time they changed locations. She spent most of her trip on the phone, at great expense, with her boyfriend back in Florida instead of focusing on the mission. Not only was her constant communication with her boyfriend a distraction to her, the entire team was frustrated and annoyed by her incessant contact with her covetous boyfriend.

Many people who come to the Philippines on mission quickly become homesick. Some have small children that they've never been away from before. Others have family members who are going through some very difficult health situations. For some, the mission trip schedule causes them to miss birthday celebrations or wedding anniversaries. It's natural to miss those whom you love, and there's nothing wrong with being homesick. It's how you deal with your homesickness that is important while on mission trips.

First of all, remember that you are going to be separated from those that you love for only a couple of weeks. Your host missionary also has family 'back home' that they may not have seen in years. They love their families as intensely as you do and communicate with them regularly, just not incessantly. Plan to limit the amount of communication to friends and family back home to a minimum. Let your friends and family know that your internet and telephone access will be severely limited and prepare them for your absence. Leave notes behind for husbands, wives, and children – one for each person for every day that you'll be absent so that the family receives word from you that requires no personal contact.

No internet service was available in our province when we first arrived in the Philippines in 1999; the closest internet service was four and a half hours away across rugged, mountainous dirt roads in Cabanatuan City. We travelled there once each month to check our e-mail and communicate with the outside world. There was also no cell phone (or home phone) service. If we absolutely needed to make a phone call, we had three phone booths inside of the Philippine Long Distance Telephone (PLDT) office. The PLDT office required that we sign in, list the number of the party we wanted to call, and they would connect us to the people we wanted to speak to when it was our turn. Once they connected the call for you, you would step into the phone booth and close the door to block out the considerable amount of street noise so that you could hear the person at the other end. With the door closed, the booth was like a sauna. You could speak for as long as you wanted once you were in the sauna/booth, which, at more than four dollars per minute wasn't long. Months would pass before I was able to speak with my parents, children or grandchildren. I'm telling you this to explain why I'm unsympathetic when a short term visitor mopes around all day after missing their morning or evening phone call home.

As short term visitors, you'll be back in the arms of your loves ones in 10-12 days. Plan not to communicate with them and celebrate each chance you're provided to communicate with them. Our teams meet each morning for breakfast at 7:00, followed by a brief period of 'team time' to discuss our plans for the day and talk about highlights from the previous day. We typically have a few minutes to fill water bottles, grab our backpacks and prepare to head out. This is not the time to race other team members to your host's computer to send e-mails, update facebook, or use Skype (or whatever other VOIP program is available for phone calls.)

I recommend that you build some specific time into the team schedule to use for communication. This will ensure that each team member is given an opportunity to communicate, and also to let folks back home know when to expect your calls or updates. Remember the time difference between your mission location and home. Here we're twelve hours ahead of Eastern Daylight Time (until daylight saving time goes into effect, when we become thirteen hours ahead.) Knowing the time difference will help you plan the best time to set aside for team communication. Mornings and evenings from 7:00–9:00 are the best times for people here to reach families on the east coast of the United States. Teams from the west coast would communicate most easily between 10:00 – 12:00 in the morning and evening.

Your family should be able to reach you in the event of an emergency. So, even if you are going to a remote region with little communication to the outside world, ask your host how the team can be contacted in the event of an emergency. But please make sure that your family (or jealous boyfriend) understands what constitutes an emergency. Accidents, serious injuries or death in the family are emergencies; report card news, engagement announcements, or soap opera updates are not. Make sure that every team member has been given emergency contact information to provide to their families before they depart.

Plan to limit the amount of time you spend each time that you're given an opportunity to communicate. Consider that other team members also need to use the same phone or computer that you're using. I have an unsecure wireless connection available at my house so that anyone with a wireless device can connect. Plan to share your communications device even if you brought your own i-pad, i-pod, i-phone, notebook/laptop computer, blackberry or raspberry. Figure out who will become your team technology guru to troubleshoot connection problems, and "NO", he may not reconfigure parameters in my router.

We hosted a visitor who connected to his family and friends using his own laptop computer through Skype every moment that we were back at my house. It was ridiculous! He wandered around the yard aiming his laptop camera at banana trees, coconut trees, my fishpond, my dogs, the food we were preparing …there wasn't a moment when he was disconnected from his friends and family. He had the audacity to announce at our team meeting one morning, "I just don't feel like I'm part of the team." It was no wonder, he was a world away while the rest of the team ate together, laughed together, and enjoyed fellowship with our Filipino brothers and sisters. It's not my job, as your host missionary, to tell you when, how long, or with whom you may communicate. Your team leader, however, should set your team's guidelines for communications before you leave home.

Another consideration regarding communications is disruption of service. While our internet provider has been reliable, our electricity supply is not. Prepare your team for the unexpected. You won't be able to communicate using the internet while our power is out.

Costly international cell phone communications may still be available during power outages, but make sure that you know the full cost of such communication. One of our visitors received a phone bill that was hundreds of dollars higher than expected the month after he got home. It seems his phone service provider in the US offered a low monthly rate, but included a costly option for incoming international calls. Know before you go.

Bring along blank CD's or DVD's (or huge flash drives) to share photos and video. A picture is worth a thousand words, but takes much longer to upload. My internet connection is quite slow by most standards, so uploading huge video files or large volumes of high quality photos is not an option while here (or most remote locations.) Set aside time near the end of the trip to gather team photos and video and share them with one another.   Teams who say they'll share these photos and videos when they get home are delusional – they don't.

Lastly, please communicate what the Lord accomplished through you, and how you were personally affected during your mission trip.   Especially to those who helped sponsor you.   Don't just post two hundred photos into an online photo bucket and send them a link.   Make this communication personal and powerful.

Absence weakens mediocre passions and increases the great ones, as the wind blows out candles and kindles fires. - François de la Rochefoucauld

Chapter Eighteen Discussion Questions

1. Have all family members been provided with emergency contact information?

2. Have you asked your host missionary about availability of internet? Phone?

3. What time of day will be set aside for the team to communicate home? What time will that be at home?

4. Have you written any notes to leave behind for your family?

5. Have you set the expectation with family and friends that communications will be limited and infrequent?

6. Are you prepared to limit your conversations to less than five minutes when communicating home so that all the other team members also have an opportunity to do so?

7. If you have a device that connects to the internet and uninterrupted Wi-Fi is available, are you willing to commit your time to the team and mission instead of spending all your 'down' time online?

8. What is your team's plan to share your photos and video?

Couples

One of the more delicate team issues happens when couples decide to travel on a mission trip together. The problem is not the romance they share - it's the amount of focus they spend on each other at the expense of the mission and the team. There's nothing wrong with married couples sharing the same bed; they've done so every night from the time that they were married. But married couples need to understand that things are different on the mission field. They need to get out of their comfort zone, interact with other team members, and realize that 'field accommodations' likely require that males room with other males and females with other females.

Let me keep the spotlight on married people for another paragraph or two. The problem isn't that they spend too much time gazing lovingly into one another's eyes. On the contrary, the challenge with married couples is that they are often too familiar with each other. A husband may have an irritating habit that his wife simply can't ignore. She's spent years training him, so she can't allow his 'backsliding' to go unchallenged without a snide comment. Combative verbal exchanges between couples may not affect their relationship in any way; they may be quite comfortable with such exchanges, but others on the team are clearly made uncomfortable by their apparent discord. Wives: other team members don't want to hear you blame your husband for forgetting the insect repellent. Husbands: neither your wife nor the remaining team members desire your rebuttal. If you and your spouse are travelling together, plan to treat one another with extra respect during the trip. Play nice with one another. Everyone else on the team will appreciate that.

We hosted a team that included a married couple who disagreed about everything. Disagreement is fine; my wife and I disagree on things quite frequently. But this couple permitted small disagreements to become loud, awkward confrontations. Other team members would quickly clear the room or find another place to go when these confrontations arose. But worse, our Filipino brothers and sisters, who absolutely avoid confrontations, were aghast at their behavior. Please, if you're married and travelling together on missions, set aside petty disagreements for the duration of the trip.

We've also hosted young married couples who were obviously still in the honeymoon stage. They swooned over each other and paid far too much attention to each other for the entire trip. Even though we'd rearrange our evangelism teams so that they could experience the style of different team members and local pastors, our honeymooners refused to be separated. They wanted to experience everything together, but their togetherness became an impediment to our team effort. One young husband became ill, and his wife became irrational in her effort to make him comfortable and speed his healing. Even though there was nothing she could do (except catch his virus), she remained with him instead of participating in the mission.

As a couple, it's exciting to serve the Lord together, especially in another culture. But I would like to offer the same advice as I would to newly married couples who are still in the honeymoon stage. When your mission team leader suggests that you partner with other team members, there's likely a reason for it. You may be unaware of it, but others may have already observed your fascination with one another taking precedence over the mission or at the expense of team unity. Agree before you travel that the mission and team unity should be placed above one another for a couple of weeks. You can share stories of what happened with your teams if you are placed in separate groups.

And please, if you have a disagreement with each other, postpone any announcement of your impending breakup until the trip is completed. International travel can be stressful. There are plenty of inconveniences and frustrations that can cause friction. Your relationship will be tested. You may not like the way the young girls smile or flirt with your boyfriend. You may like his return smile even less, but don't allow such things to impact the mission. It's the same with you, guys. Your girlfriend is special, that's why you enjoy being with her. People may introduce her as 'single' and you may not appreciate the attention she receives from other men. Get over it. Focus on the reason you've come and support one another. Your mission experience together will be remembered forever, even if your relationship doesn't survive as long.

There's another type of romance that, sadly, needs to be discussed, and that's an illicit romance, with one or both parties who are married to another person. I bring this up because it's happened here in our ministry. A married man came to the Philippines on a team that also included a young married woman. They seemed to be getting a little too "chummy,"' so the team leader suggested that they spend less time together and the young woman mocked him for even suggesting that there was anything inappropriate going on. She would say things like: *"We'd better not sit across the table from one another or we'll get another lecture."* But the team leader's perceptiveness proved correct. They had already entered into an adulterous affair before the trip and planned to use the time here in the Philippines to be together. They were eventually found out, and the man (who worked in ministry) lost his job, his wife and his children as a result. Stay away from one another if sparks start to fly - married or unmarried, the mission trip is not the time to begin a romance.

And let's face it, as a single American you're attractive as a mate to members of the opposite sex in third world nations. You represent an escape from poverty, an opportunity for a better life, and you are also attractive. And you're godly. You're perfect. Beautiful young ladies in our church have quarrelled over a young, single male missionary more than once (though it can happen just as easily with single ladies who come as missionaries.) One of our young missionaries returned home and continued to contact a young woman here in the Philippines. The relationship never 'flowered', but the young woman lost her hard-working, good-looking, godly, college-educated Filipino boyfriend as a result of the missionary's overtures. I would never even suggest that God's intended mate for you won't be found while on a mission trip.   My suggestion, however, is to focus your adoration on Jesus during the trip and postpone any romantic notions until the trip is over.

When the woman saw that the fruit of the tree was good for food and pleasing to the eye, and also desirable for gaining wisdom, she took some and she ate it. She also gave some to her husband who was with her, and he ate it. - Genesis 3:6

Chapter Nineteen Discussion Questions

1. If you are traveling with your spouse, have you graciously accepted separate accommodations?

2. Have you and your spouse discussed ways to minimize friction during the trip?

3. Even though you are a couple, have you agreed to prioritize the mission and keep the focus off of one another during the trip?

4. Is jealousy a problem in your relationship? If so, how will you deal with it on the trip?

5. Do you have any attraction towards a member of the opposite sex on your team? If so, what safeguards have you put in place to avoid any romantic overtures?

6. What should/will be your response to flirtation from local nationals during the trip?

Filipino Time

"You can't change the past, but you can ruin the present by worrying about the future" – (anonymous)

Take off your watch before you come to the Philippines because it will only become a source of frustration. When someone from our province invites you to an event that's scheduled to start at 2:00pm, you're still on time if you show up at 4:00pm. In fact, you might be the first to arrive! You'll discover that time is not as important in many places as it is in the USA.

Lack of concern for punctuality was a constant source of frustration for me during my first few months in the Philippines. I spent twenty years in the US Air Force, where punctuality wasn't an option, but a requirement. Failure to show up to work or scheduled appointments on time could result in punishment (typically fines), denial of promotion eligibility, or, if habitual, discharge.) After the Air Force I became part of a sales team, selling multimillion dollar software solutions to Fortune 500 companies. What's the possibility that we'd sell our product if we wasted the time of corporate executives by showing up late for a scheduled meeting? Zero!

Punctuality was expected from me my entire life: in school, through the military years, and as a systems consultant. It took many months for me to slow down to the pace of life here in the Philippines, so I fully understand when short term missionaries become irritated when scheduled events don't happen as planned.

I was asked to serve as a judge at a community talent contest just a few weeks after we moved to the Philippines. The event was supposed to start at 7:00 p.m., so as usual, I was in place at 6:45. When I arrived there was no stage, no sound system, no lights, and no people: I was the first (and only) person there. I returned home and went back to the site of the show at 7:45. Still there were no others. So, once again, I returned home. I worried that everyone might be waiting on me, so I returned at 8:45. A few other people had arrived, but there was still no stage, no lights, no sound system and no contestants. Out of frustration I went home and didn't return. The contest took place, but didn't begin until after 11:00pm. That's four hours late, and nobody cared! I was the only person that even noticed the time. It's simply not a big deal here.

Expect delays when attending any activity in the Philippines. Bring your Bible or something else to read if you wish to make your 'down time' more productive. Just don't become irritated or become ugly because your expectations are not being met. I went to a conference in Baguio City with leaders from a local church. The pastor, who would be driving the church van announced, "We will leave exactly at 4:30 a.m., anyone not here on time will be left behind." Then he turned to me and said, "*For you, Barry, that means seven o'clock.*"

I teach time as a stewardship issue. We're each apportioned only a certain measure of time, and we'll be held accountable before God for our use of that time. Time is a resource that is far more valuable than other resources. Your house can burn down and you can build another. Your money can be stolen, but you can acquire more. But time, once it's been spent, can never again be retrieved. I have no expectation of changing the culture here in the rural Aurora Province, but I set an example by starting events (and worship services) exactly at the announced time. Filipinos say our start time will be at 8:00 "American time", meaning that we will begin exactly at eight o'clock. I prefer to say "Christian time," suggesting that we need to be reliable, dependable, and predictable as believers.

Some cultures have no tenses in their language to represent past, present or future. And there are cultures that don't view time as progressing in a linear fashion, and clocks mean nothing. Our understanding of time may not be shared by the culture you're visiting, and you won't change their view of time during your visit. You'll need to be the one who adjusts to the local culture regarding issues of punctuality and time management. I was told by a missionary friend that Brazilians relate punctuality with success exactly the opposite the way that we think. While we associate success with a strong work ethic (punctuality included), Brazilians who are successful make it a point never to show up on time. When I lived in Hawaii it was far more laid back than life on the mainland. This frustrated Japanese tourists who were accustomed to a greater promptness and punctuality than most Americans. Their frustrations didn't change Hawaiian culture, nor is our expectation of punctuality going to alter the local concept of time when we visit other cultures. Here in the province, punctuality is relative. It's almost an art form to guess how late others will arrive at an event.

Let your team leader and your host missionary worry about logistical things. Ride when your transportation shows up. Sing when the music plays. Look for opportunities to share Jesus when you experience delays. Understand that those "down times" are not in our plans, but they may be in God's plan — divine appointments waiting to happen.

Teach us to number our days aright -- that we might gain a heart of wisdom. - Psalm 90:12

Chapter Twenty Discussion Questions

1. What will you do with any unplanned 'down time'?

2. Are you already thinking about divine appointments? Understand that they happen outside of our normal plans, so our antennas should be alerted for them when we encounter delays or unscheduled time.

3. Given the lack of concern for punctuality in many cultures, will you deal gracefully with others who have 'stolen' your valuable time?

21 Awkward Questions

I read a magazine article about a woman in Atlanta who helped her poor neighbors with groceries. She said that many of them responded to her kindness by asking for more. It was just an observation, not a judgment. In the article she was quoted as saying, "A poor person's way of saying 'thank you' is to ask for more." I've witnessed the same behavior many times. The poor here in our province have no place to turn for help; their entire extended family is also poor and the government is incapable of meeting simple infrastructure needs. So, they are truly overwhelmed when they're given a sack of rice, prenatal vitamins or assistance to buy medicine. And since they have no other place to turn for help, they return to the only source of assistance they know.

I understand that people in need will ask us for help. Sometimes their needs are great, such as emergency transport for an injured family member. And sometimes their needs are small, such as two kilos of rice to eat while they await a promised payment from a cousin returning from Manila. Whether great or small, their needs are real, and we try to assist in some small way. But, sadly, our resources fall far short, and quite often all we can offer is prayer. Learning to say 'no' is one of the most difficult aspects of ministry in an impoverished region. But we've learned how to refuse help without dismissing their need, or making them feel insignificant.

I include this information for your benefit. You will be confronted with the same needs that we encounter, and you need to prepare your response. It's not unusual for a total stranger to ask you for help. The request will begin politely, "Excuse me sir/ma'am, may I ask a favor from you?" Then you will hear a heartbreaking story with an attached plea for your financial assistance. The stories are real, and the need is legitimate. But you need to prepare your response in advance. What will you say when an elderly woman approaches you, holds your hands, looks you in the eyes and tearfully begs you to help her husband with cancer? What is your response to the young woman who is holding a limp baby with a high fever who asks for your help? How will you respond to a man who tells you he can't afford to send his daughter to school? You'll have to respond to them – what will you say?

Many short term missionaries open their hearts and reach immediately for their wallets when they are presented with such needs. They pull out a wad of bills and give generously to help meet the need. There's nothing wrong with that, except that it invites a flood of additional requests (to teammates as well) from neighbors, family members, and anyone else who may have witnessed or heard about the generous gift. Unless you have very deep pockets, at some point you'll need to politely refuse. You don't need to explain your financial situation back home or tell them how much you paid for airfare just to get here; simply tell them that you are unable to help and offer to pray with them.

We serve a God who entrusts us with His resources. We're required to faithfully manage all finances entrusted to us; they belong to God, and we will have to give an account of what we did with the Lord's money (not just ten percent, but everything we were given to manage.) I could stand before the judgment throne of Christ and justify using the Lord's money to help people in need. Any righteous use of his resources can be justified. But there are both good and better uses of money. When we respond to any need we need to ask ourselves, "Is this the best use for this money?" We can always justify money spent to help with a righteous cause as 'good' use of the money. But if we select the need we wish to help with (instead of responding to needs that come to us), we may be able to claim that the money was 'better' spent. But we should always be examining the 'best' use of the Lord's money.

Corruption is systemic in the Philippines and in many other nations around the world. People from corrupt cultures naturally assume that missionaries behave the same way as government employees, and the leadership of other aid agencies. They presume that we're just like everyone else, skimming some of the money for ourselves that was intended for others. It's a natural distrust, derived from experience. They've never encountered people who are unwilling to compromise their principles for money.

It's frustrating that we're also viewed as corrupt by the very people we assist. We advertise on our website that a donation of $80.00 will sponsor a child to school for an entire year; it covers the cost of school uniform, shoes, a backpack filled with school supplies and helps cover tuition fees. Families have asked us to provide them with $80.00 in cash (knowing from our website that $80.00 is the amount of money we receive to assist their children.) They tell us that they could better manage their own child's school expenses with that money. We know better than to provide cash. A drunken father may use it to entertain his drinking buddies. Or the household may use it for medicine, food, clothing or other important needs that are unrelated to education. We want to make sure that the money donated for education is used for education. When we refuse to provide them with cash, they assume that we're 'skimming' money from their child's account. Nothing could be further from the truth. In fact, we use money from our general funds to cover the cost of printed photos, postage, fuel for delivery of items, etc. We even adjust the amount of supplies that each student receives based on the current exchange rate so that we can maximize the benefit to each child. But distrust is endemic; we earn the trust of those who witness how we operate, but some will always view us through the same cynical lense that they use to view everyone else.

The reason that you need to understand this is that you may be asked to help people circumvent processes that have been put in place by your host missionary. One of our board members, our Director of Education, visits the Philippines frequently. While visiting a local elementary school, the principal took her aside, and in hushed tones, suggested that it would be best to channel money for 'her' students directly through her. What she was implying is that she would be a better steward of that money than we are. The reality is that she wanted her cut of the money, and our current processes don't permit any of it to be siphoned off to school administrators. But even if she was able to provide 100% of the money to the students, God wouldn't receive the glory. We use the student sponsorships, medical assistance, disaster response, and all of the benevolence projects as platforms to share the Gospel of Jesus Christ. Our goal isn't just to assist poor families by lifting their financial burden; it's to make Christ known. The cause of Christ would suffer if people could manage to find a 'back door', obtaining benefits without going through established processes.

Let people know that you support your host missionary's efforts, and that you will work through their established policies and processes.   It will even help you if or when you're approached for money. We know many of the families here in the area, and can vouch for those who are in need. We can also tell you who are drug addicts and drunks, or have a reputation as cheats and thieves. Rely on your host missionary to guide you when it comes to matters of helping others in the community.

Vincent and Charity are great folks from our home church in Savannah.   Charity called me one day to express concern over a letter she received from the Philippines. She wanted to know why we had given out her address to someone here in the Philippines without asking her permission. She received a long letter, addressed to her and her husband by name, asking for financial help. I assured her that we would never provide her address to anyone here, and asked if they might have included their names or address in a shoebox that they packed to send here with others from our church. She said that they had, in fact, included their names on a note in the shoebox, but not their address. Evidently the family that received their shoebox put two and two together; they knew that the team was from Savannah, GA and they had the full names of the people that sent them the shoebox.   A quick Google search at an internet café likely provided them with the address and zip code.

People will ask you for your contact information while you're here in the Philippines. Decide in advance whether you want to provide it to just anyone.   There may be some people in the church here that you would love to communicate with, but you may not wish to provide personal information to the drunken teenager on the corner who staggered to the Jeep to ask how he could reach you in America. I suggest that you have some team cards printed out that provide the church address instead of personal addresses.   It can contain the church website, generic e-mail account, facebook page, phone number, etc.   You can write your name on the cards and give them to strangers who ask for personal information.

Filipinos ask some intensely personal questions, even when you're strangers. I've been asked many times "What is your income?" They don't want to know the source of my income, they want to know the amount. The follow up question is always, "How much is that in pesos?"   I was taken aback by such questions when I first moved here, and provided truthful answers to some very personal questions simply because I was asked to do so. Now, when asked such questions I reply, "That's quite personal and it isn't information that I wish to share." It's not rude, but direct and to the point. And it usually, though not always, prevents personal follow-up questions.

Understand that, as a missionary, people may ask for your help. They may ask some intensely personal questions. They will ask for your address, e-mail address, and if you will become their friend on facebook. Use your judgment in such matters, but rely on your host missionary to guide you in these matters.

Blessed are the merciful, for they will be shown mercy. – Matthew 5:7

Chapter Twenty One Discussion Questions

1. Will you prepare some calling cards to hand out to people who request your contact information?

2. Instead of saying 'no', what will you say when asked for specific assistance.

3. If you decide to assist a specific individual or family, will you do so through your host missionary?

4. How will you respond if asked to circumvent giving through the local ministry? (Send it directly to me, not through them.)

5. Who will receive the glory when you give, God or you?

6. How will you answer intensely personal questions? (What is your income by the way?)

Can I stay?

Some feel the thrill, others don't.   There's an excitement for many that's hard to contain when they experience a new culture. They revel in the people, the language, the food, the customs, the scenery; everything seems so alive. However, with all its magnificence and glory, there's one problem: there are some who are not ready to leave when it's time for the team to return home. Not only do they want to stay, but they begin making arrangements to remain behind. And if those plans won't work, they plan to return as quickly as possible. They're captivated by the place and culture and willing to abandon everything else to remain among these new people that they grew quickly to love in this strange and exotic land. This is called the"honeymoon stage" of missions.

"During the early days or months of living in another culture, while still in "vacation mode," a person experiences interest, fascination, joy, and enthusiasm living in another culture. This may last for days, weeks, or even months. However, when the inevitable difficulties with language, people, housing, and food arise, people may become critical, frustrated, resentful, and angry. Simple tasks become daunting challenges, and disillusionment sets in." [ii]

Please notice that the excitement experienced by people in this cultural"honeymoon stage" has nothing to do with ministry. In every case, those who desire to remain here in the Philippines or return 'in a month or so' were motivated by something more personal. They desired more of the culture, the people, the food, or the scenery. None of them showed any particular interest in serving Christ. In most cases, their intense desire to stay was merely nothing more than a fascination with this culture. For this reason I ask team leaders to enforce team integrity. I don't want anyone coming early or remaining behind when the team goes home.

Once the honeymoon stage is over and disillusionment sets in, expect frustration. Expect corruption and bureaucracy getting your visa extended. You'll experience lengthy delays on commercial busses, which are uncomfortably filled beyond capacity. (They also won't stop at the mall and wait while you shop for souvenirs.) Those who stay will no doubt discover what five consecutive days without electricity feels like. The humidity increases and mosquitoes seem thicker. They'll start to crave a Starbuck's coffee, a slice of Papa John's pizza, or the chance to watch a football game on TV, until they realize that it isn't going to happen. They'll discover that none of the stores in town sell pants in your size, and they'll continually be amazed that the only hardware store in town *never* has what you need. Disposable razors, cold beverages, or guitar strings are not readily available. It's clear that people are reaching the point of disillusionment when they say, "Is it possible that I can get a meal here without any rice?" For some it happens within two weeks. My suggestion is this: Deal with it, and think of me when you get your milkshake, steak, or pizza at the airport (just don't include it in your Facebook status update for me to see.)

Some people travel to the Philippines with the team, but since they're already halfway around the world, they decide to visit a neighboring country at a fraction of what it would cost to get there from the United States. So, instead of returning with the team, they opt to visit Thailand, Japan, Korea or China. I'm unaffected by this, though I may spend an extra day or two in Manila to make sure that all our visitors make it safely out of the Philippines. But I've seen that it can also change team dynamics, especially when a member leaves a day or two before the other team members are scheduled to depart. There's a letdown, almost a meltdown, on the team. They sense the end of the trip and begin to focus on going home instead of on remaining mission opportunities.

There may also be liability issues if those who came with your team fall into misfortune during their side trip. Make sure that your insurance covers members separated from the team, and ensure that their policy covers them until they arrive home.

Our policy is to host only teams, not individuals. We host mission teams for as many as ten weeks each year. This means that twenty percent of our time each year is spent working directly with our short-term missionaries. We take a bus to Manila the day before they arrive to make sure that their hotel and transportation arrangements are taken care of properly. We greet them at the Manila airport and travel with them to the province. We eat with them, sleep on the same floors with them, and work side-by-side with them in every mission activity. And we travel back to Manila with them to make sure that they get safely to the airport.

Our pastors do the same for each team. They set aside every other activity to assist as drivers, translators, and to provide our teams with whatever they need. When the teams return home, we want our pastors to do the same. They make themselves available from 6:00 a.m. until late in the evening for ten weeks each year, rarely seeing their wives or children during team visits. When the teams go home, as the host missionary, we desire our pastors to return to their families and ministry, not to feel obligated assisting someone who invited himself to stay.

Having organized several mission trips, I'm keenly aware that some people desperately want to come, but the scheduled dates prove impossible. I don't set the dates for team visits; I just make sure that they don't overlap with plans from another team. I can offer to put you in touch with other teams coming here, but your best bet is to wait for your next church mission trip. Or let me offer a radical solution: skip this year's trip, but send along the cost of your airfare. That amount of money can support a pastor and his family here for the next year and a half.

Pray as a team, prepare as a team, travel as a team, work as a team, and return as a team.

I charge you, in the sight of God and Christ Jesus and the elect angels, to keep these instructions without partiality, and to do nothing out of favoritism. - 1Timothy 5:21

Chapter Twenty Two Discussion Questions

1. Have you spent any time in another culture? Describe that experience?

2. Do you anticipate being fascinated or frustrated on your mission trip? Or both? Explain why.

3. What is most likely to cause you frustration on the trip?

4. How would you counsel a team member who wishes to remain behind or return as soon as possible to your mission location?

5. Are all your team members planning to arrive and depart together?

23   **Become a Body Builder**

I'm a body builder, but you'd never guess by looking at me. I don't lift weights or do callisthenic workouts; that's not the type of body builder I'm talking about. I'm talking about strengthening the Body of Christ, building inter-denominational understanding and cooperation.

Denominational allegiance is much like allegiance to a nation; 'my' nation is elevated over all others, and, consequently, all other nations become, consciously or subconsciously, inferior. We violate the Body of Christ when we view our faith as superior to the faith of our Christian brothers and sisters. This is not to say that we set aside our doctrinal beliefs because others believe differently. We do no such thing! But we may be required to work cooperatively with other Christians of different flavors while on mission trips.

Respect the denomination of your host missionary! If your host doesn't believe in faith healing, don't lay hands on the sick and"heal them in the name of Jesus." If your host missionary doesn't speak in tongues, refrain from doing so while working in his ministry.

Accept that your host missionary has a"males only"' policy for preaching and baptizing. And please refrain from teaching anything controversial (meaning any doctrine that strays from that of your host missionary.) This is important: as short-term visitors we don't want to confuse new believers entrusted to your host. Know the doctrine of your host before you travel. Not all missionaries are ultra-conservative, but some are, and they are sensitive to things that you view as *permissible*. Have your team leader describe your host and his doctrine in as much detail as possible during your planning stage.

We invited a Pentecostal pastor to participate with a group of Southern Baptists on one trip, and the mixture was toxic. The pastor was socially delightful, but he showed little reverence for preserving Baptist doctrine within a Baptist church. His charismatic ways, particularly one 'healing service', caused confusion and a bit of needless frustration. As believers, we have enough in common to remain unified for a week or two. There's no need to behave like party-line politicians; be willing to bend and cooperate for the benefit of the ministry. Yield to the doctrinal belief of your host missionary.

For we were all baptized by one Spirit into one body – whether Jews or Greeks, slaves or free – and we were all given the one Spirit to drink. – 1 Corinthians 12: 13

Chapter Twenty Three Discussion Questions

1. Do you know the doctrinal beliefs and worship style of your host missionary?

2. Is your team interdenominational? If so, have you discussed how to avoid controversy or confusion because of the differences in beliefs?

3. Will you be able to support your host even though you disagree with their teachings (such as women must wear dresses or skirts, or only men are permitted to speak during worship)?

4. What can be done to unify teams that hold differing beliefs?

24 Enslaving your host missionary

A man was touched by the deep need of a family he encountered during evangelism visits the previous day and asked us to buy and deliver a sack of rice and 'fifty dollar's worth' of groceries to the family.   He wanted to deliver the groceries in person.   So we dispatched one of our pastors to the market to purchase the rice and groceries.   He returned and picked up our visitor and they went to the home, which is about 45 minutes away. Nobody was home, so they returned to our house with the groceries.   A second trip was made the following day with the same result, and we were left with the rice and groceries to deliver after the team departed.   Our visitor's heart was in the right place, but his insistence on being present for the delivery consumed 10% of his time here and it took away one of our pastor/translators from his responsibilities to the rest of the team.

Please remember the reason that you're traveling to another country is to assist your host missionary, not to have them help you with personal projects. These 'personal projects' typically arise when someone touches your heart. These are noble gestures of love, expressions of generosity that spring from your desire to help someone in need. And because of that, your host will unlikely say "no." But please understand that each of these requests takes resources and focus away from planned ministry activities.

This is not about me; I'm strong enough to say no. I'll offer alternatives if I feel that a request will place an unreasonable burden on our ministry. But many missionaries may be unable to refuse such requests. And, as a result of their kindness, they incur ongoing obligations. Let me explain with some real examples of such requests.

Another missionary arrived with personalized gifts for fifteen students that were sponsored by her Sunday school class. She promised the class that she would get pictures of each of the children as she visited. She didn't realize when she made that promise how difficult it would be to fulfill. Nobody was home at the first house, so we went to the next closest child's home (which was about six miles away.) The parents were home, but the sponsored student was not. She didn't want to leave the gifts with the girl's parents; she'd promised pictures of the kids and insisted that we track them down. This 'simple' request took us three full days. And two of the students were never found home, so we were left with the responsibility to deliver two gifts and obtain photos of the sponsored students once the team departed. Her heart was in the right place; she wanted to bless

the sponsored students and provide feedback to her Sunday school

class. But her insistence on being part of the photos with the children

consumed 30% of her time here in the Philippines. It also pulled

resources (a vehicle and a pastor) away from the team's planned

ministry activities.

One of our pastors admired a study Bible carried by one of our

missionaries. Our missionary realized that she had plenty of leftover

pesos as we headed to the airport and gave us money to purchase

the same study Bible for our pastor. This *simple* request required two

full days of searching every known resource in Manila. It cost us an

extra night's hotel bill and more than twenty dollars in taxi fare as we

went from Church Strengthening Ministries, to the Philippine Bible

League, to every Christian book store we could find. We never found

the Bible here in the Philippines and had to arrange for another visitor

to bring the Bible from the U.S. several months later. Again, her

heart was in the right place, but she unknowingly burdened us to

obtain it.

A couple that we love encountered a young girl here, fell in

love with her, and decided to adopt her. They enlisted our help to

arrange an adoption attorney and process the paperwork for them

here in the Philippines, which proved to be a monumental

undertaking. This request required us to take multiple trips to Cabanatuan, Manila, and Baler for various tasks. And we remain willing to do whatever we can to assist - we really want to see this young girl become part of this incredible family. The process has now taken years, and the girl is now too old to be adopted. They are still trying to obtain a student visa to bring her to the United States. They've done most of the research and use us to accomplish tasks that require a presence here. Unless you have a very close relationship with your host missionary, requests of this kind would be considered unreasonable.

Three student sponsors have asked us to provide daily transportation for their students, who live in remote locations that are quite far from their respective schools. We now have an ongoing obligation to pay three drivers each week to fulfill this request. Keeping track of the payments, reminding the sponsors when they owe additional money, and paying the drivers has taken more effort than we considered when we agreed to it.

An elderly woman, responsible for caring for four grandchildren, was having chest pains when we went to her house on a visit. One of our missionaries promised to pay for her tests and treatment and asked us to take care of it for him. He instructed us to let him know what it cost, and he'd take care of the financial burden.

Her condition turned out to be quite serious and has required her to take several trips to Cabanatuan for further diagnosis and treatment. Keeping up with her situation, needs, and financial expenses has not been simple. Again, this was an act of love and compassion – how could we possibly refuse such assistance?

You get the picture. The people being helped are exceedingly grateful for your kindness, but without knowing it, you've placed your host missionary in an awkward position. Neighbors who witness your act of kindness will visit your host to ask for rice, groceries, or medical care – after all, they witnessed you give these things to their neighbor. If excluded, some will become jealous and hold grudges. They're also in need, with children to feed and send to school, and their medical needs are even more serious than the woman we brought to Cabanatuan.   And six of the seven local pastors may secretly harbor resentment because only the one was given an expensive study Bible.

Please don't misunderstand me; I don't want to discourage giving, but we all need to realize that there's a right way and a wrong way to help people in need. You may have promised to get some photos of your friend's sponsored children, but there's no need to have them pose with the groceries. "Could you sit on the sack of rice, honey, and hold the gift box next to your face while I take another picture?" Don't take away their dignity – just give them the gift. The more fanfare required of the recipient, the less dignity you bestow them. You'll see from our ministry website that I'm also guilty of snapping photos and videotaping as assistance is rendered. But I do it as unobtrusively as possible, without asking for retakes, additional shots, or requiring anyone to pose.

There's also a right time and a wrong time for giving. Unless you absolutely have to participate in person, consider allowing a local pastor to be the one who provides your gift. He can use the opportunity to establish a relationship with the recipient family and can bring glory to God through your gift. And each request to purchase and deliver something requires effort from one of our pastors/workers. As a result we have one less translator, one less driver, and one less participant in the ministry that you've come to assist.

I can spend far more time on this topic, but won't. When you feel compelled to help someone in need, do so rationally, not just emotionally. And do it in a manner that strengthens the ministry, gives glory to God, and retains the dignity of the recipient.

[1] Be careful not to do your 'acts of righteousness' before men, to be seen by them. If you do, you will have no reward from your Father in heaven. [2] So when you give to the needy, do not announce it with trumpets, as the hypocrites do in the synagogues and on the streets, to be honored by men. I tell you they have received their reward in full. [3] But when you give to the needy, do not let your left hand know what your right hand is doing, [4] so that your giving may be in secret. Then your Father, who sees what is done in secret, will reward you. – Matthew 6:1-4

Chapter Twenty Four Discussion Questions

1. How can you avoid taking away the dignity of people who are being assisted?

2. Are you willing to let a local pastor deliver items to people who have touched your heart after the team has returned home instead of doing it personally during the mission trip?

3. What's the difference between emotional and rational giving?

4. List ways you can avoid using your host missionary to fulfill personal tasks for you once you have returned home.

25 Falling Coconuts

A coconut from a tree on my property hit Esmeraldo Antonio squarely atop his head and he immediately buckled to the ground. His companions carried him, unconscious and bleeding from his nose and ears, to my garage. A huge gash on the top of his head gushed blood and added panic to the sense of urgency. Esmeraldo needed immediate medical attention, but the harvesters piled all of the coconuts on my driveway, blocking my truck from moving. They carried him to the street in my wheelbarrow, loaded him into a tricycle and drove him to the local clinic while I created a path to remove the truck.

As we drove to the clinic to check on Mr. Antonio, several men in a tricycle waved us down and we stopped to find out how he was doing. I was shocked to find Esmeraldo with them, now conscious and talking. The clinic released him without looking for internal injuries using an X-ray or CT scan. He had stitches, a head bandage, and a prescription for pain medicine (which we provided for him.) The clinic just sent him home. There was no concern about his brain swelling, or about the cause of the blood dripping from his ears. Esmeraldo Antonio, fortunately, has fully recovered and is fortunate to be alive!

The reason that I relate this story is to validate the internet claim that you are more likely to die from a falling coconut than from a shark attack. I own a single hectare of coconut land, and have personally witnessed the kind of damage that falling coconuts cause. If you consider the fact that I have only a single hectare of coconuts, and that there are millions of hectares of coconuts in the world, it's likely that tens of thousands of people are hit by falling coconuts each year. The most common estimate found on the internet suggests that around 150 people are killed each year from falling coconuts. I contend that the number is substantially higher, not lower.

Crocodiles, for whatever reason, never made my list of things to worry about here in Philippines, but they do now. A world record, twenty one foot, 2370 pound salt water crocodile was captured alive in Agusan del Sur this week. It took one hundred villagers to pull it to the edge of the stream and a crane to lift it from the water! Nothing could ruin a baptism service at the river more than a crocodile attack.

How many North Americans consider the threat of crocodiles or falling coconuts in their planning? Or what about drunk men with machetes? Several men in my neighborhood have been killed by drunks with machetes during the time that we've lived here. How many mission team leaders warn about that threat? You and I may be oblivious to safety threats that are common knowledge to people in your host nation. Just because you're unacquainted with a threat doesn't make it less real. Even if it seems ludicrous at the time, please listen to your host missionary when asked to step out from beneath a coconut tree, or to remain in the 'compound' after dark. They have your best interest at heart.

Drunkenness is a serious problem here in the Philippines. In most rural areas there are no sobriety programs to help people overcome their addictions to drugs or alcohol. It's hard to overcome alcoholism when your best friends, neighbors, and family members are also alcoholics. You can't remain at home without being surrounded by people who encourage you to drink with them. Consequently, we encounter drunks at every hour of the day. The majority gathers in the late afternoon or evening when their work is done, and they're typically hospitable and invite you to join them. But there's frequently a 'mean drunk' in the group, who becomes confrontational just because you refused the offer to join them. No amount of reason will persuade him that you meant no harm or that you're on a tight schedule and need to return to join the rest of your team. In such cases just smile and remain silent. Allow your translator to speak for you. They've likely encountered such situations many times before and will know how to appease a mean drunk. You wouldn't kick a beehive, nor should you debate with (and risk enraging) an angry drunk. Allow your translator to offer conciliatory words and move away quickly. And go far enough away that he will not follow you.

There are psychopathic personalities in every culture – people who feel no guilt or remorse for things that they do to others. They have an abnormal lack of empathy and they are typically amoral and antisocial. Robert Hare is one of the world's most prominent researchers of Antisocial Personality Disorder (APD). Hare asserts that approximately one percent of the world's population may, in fact, have psychopathic personalities.[iii] If he's correct, that means that we have more than sixty million people on this planet who are incapable of guilt or remorse. I don't believe that there are any 'unredeemable souls', but God's help is clearly required when dealing with people who are incapable of feeling guilt or remorse. Christopher J. Patrick in his 'Handbook of Psychopathy' asserts that psychopathy can be neither cured nor effectively treated. There are no available medications that can instill sympathy. [iv]

A young man in our neighborhood called "Buko" is the reason I'm taking your time to discuss social disorders. He's attempted to kill other people in the neighborhood, but, to our knowledge, hasn't yet succeeded. He intentionally disrupts worship services with profanity-laced outbursts, and refuses to leave when confronted by church elders. The police have been forced to carry him away from our church. Buko wants people to fear him. He thrives on it. If the researches are right, there are people like Buko in virtually every community on planet earth. They need our prayers, and we need to demonstrate grace when dealing with them. Evil spirits and bad characters give us the opportunity to 'turn the other cheek' and allow the character of Christ to be demonstrated. Even if we are unable to reach Buko, others may be attracted to Christ by what they've seen of Him in us.

The same applies to people with other mental disorders. You won't find many people with serious mental illness walking the streets of your home town. Mental illnesses in the US are treated, and those who require it are institutionalized. Not so here. The kids in our neighborhood throw rocks at the 'crazy lady' when she comes around, and she returns fire with larger rocks. She may wear clothes or walk around entirely naked. She stands in the road and refuses to let traffic pass. Everyone knows that she has a problem, but they also know her family doesn't have any money to help her. It's the same with many, many people here. You may meet them and never know it (because your translator won't tell you that the smiling, sweet old lady in front of you said that she was going to 'pull your teeth, pound them into powder, snort the powder, and steal your strength.')

It's difficult to plan a godly response to evil acts from people like Buko. And each situation will dictate how we respond when confronted by a mean drunk. Aside from asking the Lord for help, it's difficult to deal with seriously mentally impaired people. But there are common sense safety precautions that we need to consider. Just because you're on a mission trip doesn't mean that you are impervious to serious injury or death. You may not have seatbelts to wear, but you can ride inside a vehicle instead of on the top. You can avoid touching animals. You can refrain from diving into murky water. And you can avoid the shade of coconut trees.

The horse is made ready for the day of battle, but victory rests with the Lord. - Proverbs 21:31

Chapter Twenty Five Discussion Questions

1. Do a quick danger assessment: what dangers are unique to the mission environment where you are headed?

2. What is the proper response when confronted by a mean drunk or psychopath?

3. Are you prepared, literally, to 'turn the other cheek'?

Be alert: severe mental disorders can cause extreme and unusual behaviors. Discuss ways that you might deal with people who are affected by extreme mental illness.

26 Supertyphoon

Helicopters swooped into the field next to the plaza during our worship service, and the congregation became transfixed on the action. Soldiers carrying large caliber weapons and mortars ran to the first helicopter as it landed. As soon as they lifted off the next helicopter landed, loading dozens of camouflaged soldiers. It was impossible to concentrate on worship with the noise of the rotors and the roar of the powerful engines. The pounding, thumping pulses faded, but were audible for several minutes after they left.

Our pastor couldn't remember where he left off, and none of us could help him. We all wondered what was happening with the soldiers. Where were they going in such hurry? Why were they so heavily armed? What were they responding to? The incident served to remind me that we live in a place of instability. And it reminded me that we're not in control. We're thrust into some situations that we'd rather avoid, but we simply make the best of our circumstances. When our plans are disrupted, we breathe deeply, laugh at the circumstance, then resume as best we can.

The electrical power supply here (and in many other places you may go) is unreliable. We've conducted Bible studies and prayer meetings by candle light, flashlight, or lights from cell phones. There's no convenient time for power to go out. We need water to bathe, cook, clean and flush toilets. The heat becomes hard to bear without an electric fan. We lose the ability to communicate via the internet, and after a day or two the cell phones can no longer be recharged. Frequent power outages here serve to remind me how blessed I am. We cheer when our electric fans begin to spin again, but many of my neighbors don't even notice. They have no electric fan. They don't applaud when the electric water pump comes on so they can flush the toilet because they have neither of those things . We eagerly reboot our router and computers and race back to the Internet, leaving behind those who can only dream of such things. We are blessed.

My fascination with storms has been moderated because my neighbors are so severely impacted by flooding and strong winds. Secretly I want to experience a Category 5 typhoon, but I pity my neighbors when we have storms. They can't dry their rice harvest when it rains, and a stationary low pressure area can ruin their crop. Everything they own is invested in each crop; the seed, fertilizer, and labor are usually paid off after the crop is sold. So storms often mean financial ruin. Typhoon strength winds rip off their roofs, scatter their livestock, and damage their crops.

Typhoons are possible here in any month of the year, but are most frequent between July and December. July is our most active month, but the strongest storms typically arrive in October and November. The reason I tell you this is to prepare you in advance. The weather is beyond our control, so there's no guarantee that you'll avoid a typhoon if you come here. A typhoon may delay your arrival or departure (costing you extra hotel nights). It may trap you on this side of the Sierra Madre Mountains due to flooding and landslides (which can take weeks to clear.) It may change your planned ministry, or prevent you from doing what you came to do.

We should accept that many things are out of our control: power outages, typhoons, earthquakes, insurgencies or war. Everyone wants to return home as scheduled, but don't let your inflexible schedule place you in danger. Instead of crossing the mountains during periods of heavy landslides, plan to remain a few extra days. Better safe than sorry. It's the same with earthquakes – don't be on the first bus to traverse bridges and overpasses that may have been compromised by the tremor. Stay an extra day. People will understand if a natural disaster has delayed your return. You may wish to keep an eye on approaching storms so that you can return to civilization before they arrive. I can say with certainty that you will be stuck here for at least a couple of days if a typhoon strikes. Even if there are no landslides, a steep, muddy curve called 'the horseshoe' will be impossible to navigate safely.

Remember that our plans are secondary to God's plans. You may experience unexpected interruptions even without typhoons and earthquakes. Plan for things that are known, but prepare for the unknown. Uncertainty is a blessing from God. We are able to lean on the Lord and learn to trust Him more during times of insecurity. Use times of adversity to bless others.

Now I want you to know, brothers and sisters, that what has happened to me has actually served to advance the gospel. - Philippians 1:12

Chapter Twenty Six Discussion Questions

1. List natural disasters that are possible in the nation you are visiting?

2. Is the national government considered to be strong and stable? How radical are anti-government forces in the region you will visit?

3. If thrust into a chaotic situation, does your team have a plan in place to ensure that you remain safe?

4. Do you know how to change your airline tickets if the need arises?

27 Mother Falls

Some mission teams plan to work every day of their trip without a break. This is especially true of medical teams, knowing that hundreds of suffering people wait patiently for them each day. They say that they cannot sacrifice a day off and must maximize their effort on the mission field. They think that it's frivolous to take a day off considering the expense, length of travel, and preparation for the trip. Besides, they need to dispense all of the medicine that they brought along. But my experience says otherwise. Teams need some time to relax, see the sights, and renew their strength.

Frustrations tend to surface when teams refuse to take any time off. They seem more easily irritated over small problems and they tend to disagree more openly. Nobody wants to be the one to admit that they want, or need, a down day. Everyone nods their heads in agreement when someone proposes that the team press forward without a break. After nine or ten long days without a break, however, teams begin to lose their mental focus. They become complacent, demonstrated first by their lack of punctuality. Team members start skipping meals with the team. Some choose to sleep in and skip breakfast. Departures begin later in the morning, and teams return earlier in the afternoon. It's especially evident with the exchange of sarcastic remarks, mean-spirited humor, and vicious pranks. You can even measure frustration by the increase of complaints veiled as suggestions.

But let me encourage you to take a day off and enjoy some recreation time with one another. Bring along the local pastors and their families and some of your brothers and sisters who have been serving as your translators. Remember, however, no matter where you go, you are still on mission. My favorite place to bring visitors is to Kaunayan Falls. It's only half an hour away, requires no hiking, and offers a place of serenity and extraordinary beauty. And we've led many people to the Lord while visiting the falls during our 'day off'. On two different trips we've baptized truant students who accepted Christ while we were at the waterfall. We invited them to join us for lunch, and took the time to share Jesus with them. We've even led a group of men who were half finished with a liter bottle of gin in prayer. These unexpected, unplanned, divine appointments will long be remembered.

Some teams have experienced difficulty getting re-motivated when they take a day off with only a day or two remaining on their trip.

We've waited until the final day a couple of times, but it creates extra anxiety for people like me, who worry about all the things that need to be done before being ready to leave. It's up to your team leader whether you take time off during the trip, and where you include it in your schedule. But consider this – it's not just your time off. I hosted five mission teams last year. That's ten weeks of time with only five days off. It would have been ten weeks without a day off if they failed to build a day off into their schedule.   This issue also affects our pastors and translators. They give 100% of their time to be with the team during visits. Please consider the people here when you plan your schedule.

My neighbor hurried to my house one afternoon to tell me that some American doctors were treating people at our town plaza, so I drove to town to meet them. They were easy to locate, as they were surrounded by about a thousand people waiting for treatment. I found three doctors and four nurses from Michigan, much too busy to talk with me, who looked completely exhausted. I learned that they were on the twelfth day of their trip and that they'd been working an average of fifteen hours each day, sleeping only in the vans between destinations. They'd been in six towns in eleven days, and had just traveled nine hours to get here. And they were scheduled to fly back to the U.S. from Manila (eight hours away from here) the next morning.

I brought them some bottled water, and spoke with two of the doctors. They had no idea that they were only a few miles away from one of the most beautiful beaches on the planet, and I coaxed them into a quick trip to the beach. It took us fifteen minutes to get to the beach, five minutes for them to take some photos and obtain video, and fifteen minutes to get back to the town plaza. They explained that our brief trip to the beach had been their only break during the entire trip.

Break? I've spent more time eating a bowl of cereal than it took for our swift trip to the beach. It wasn't much of a break, but I was assured that it was the most time off they'd enjoyed during their entire trip to the Philippines. Both doctors affirmed that it was a spectacular relief just to stand near the beach for a few moments. There was no way that their team could possibly treat all of the patients gathered in that huge crowd at the plaza. They likely treated less than twenty percent of them. In the grand scheme of things, it matters very little whether they were able to treat 96 people that afternoon and evening or only eighty nine people. I understand that seven people would be left out, but hundreds more were turned away when it was time for them to leave.

When it's time to eat lunch, someone has to tell the waiting crowd to go home and return later. And when it's time to call it a day, someone has to tell them to come back again in the morning. And on the last day someone has to tell them, "Sorry, but we've run out of time and you won't be seen by our doctors." (We save vitamins to give to those people.) Our efforts often seem inconsequential, mere band-aid fixes. We're frequently overwhelmed with needs that we simply can't meet. Some conditions are beyond our ability to treat. And there are too many patients to be seen. And that's precisely why we need to remind ourselves why we're here. We can repair broken bodies, but not all of them. Our most important team contribution, however, isn't medical – we've been given the opportunity to change eternity for some who come to be healed!

The world won't become a better place because you skipped a day of recreation and kept your noses to the grindstone. Sure, you'll apply more band-aids if you focus only on the mission for which you came. But it's possible that the Lord has prepared some divine appointments for you on your "day off." Allow the Lord to work through you in unexpected ways.   If you over-schedule your trip, you may miss something that God has planned for you that's not in your plan.   Open your schedule a bit, and remain alert to divine appointments.

Unless everyone on your team is young, athletic and adventurous, you wouldn't want to hike into the mountains to swim at the Mother Falls. There are narrow ledges with steep drops, swift streams to traverse, and climbing is required. One of our most beloved visitors is Miss Betty, who is now 85-years-old. Miss Betty has recently had both of her knees replaced and just returned to the Philippines for her third trip. It would be sinful to leave her behind while only the healthy members of the team (with good balance) hiked into the mountains to enjoy the magnificent Mother Falls. Team leaders should work with the host missionary to plan recreation activities so that everyone is able to participate (including the host pastors and their families.) Some of the invited locals may have small children to carry. They'll likely be the ones who will carry all of your food, pots and pans and cooking utensils needed to prepare your meals. Choose locations that are both accessible and safe.

As much as I enjoy Kaunayan Falls, I know that there are occasional skirmishes between rebel forces and government soldiers in that area. Twice we've had to cancel our plans to go there due to battles near the falls. One team wanted to take a vote to decide whether they should risk a trip to the falls. Even if everyone on the team is willing to 'chance it', please heed the advice of your host missionary.

A friend of mine remained behind after the mission team went home.   He wanted to see more of the area and experience more of the culture.   He was invited by some of my Ilonggot (former headhunter tribe) friends to hike to a waterfall in the mountains on tribal land.   I advised against it because I know a man who was kidnapped and held for ransom while hiking in the same region, and he was a Filipino pastor!   Imagine how much more prized an American hostage would be.   My friend assured me that he was willing to take the risk.   But think about it – the risk is not just his! What's the chance that we would *ever* get visitors to come here again if one of the missionaries from our church was kidnapped and held for ransom? My friend wasn't just risking his own safety – he was risking the future of our ministry in order to experience adventure.   Accept the advice of your host missionary, even when you feel that you're being 'overprotected.'

Enjoy some 'down' time with one another during your trip, and include those who serve alongside you as you minister to others. Ministry is all about relationships.

Consequently you are no longer foreigners and aliens, but fellow citizens with God's people and members of God's household. - Ephesians 2:19

Chapter Twenty Seven Discussion Questions

1. Has your team planned for a day off during the trip?

2. Are your team members physically capable of participating in your planned activities?

3. What circumstances are likely to cause frustration and stress?

4. How can you minimize stress during the trip? How will you deal with moments of stress?

5. Are there sufficient breaks planned?

6. Have you invited the local pastors and their families (interpreters and other co-laborers as well) to join you on your excursion day?

7. Are there any planned activities that might put the local ministry at risk?

28 Am I still 'colored'?

A few years ago an elderly Filipino approached me and, speaking excellent English, explained that he had once worked in Pensacola, Florida. It was in the early 1950s, before I was born. He was curious about whether or not he would still be considered to be "colored" if he were to return to America. During his visit he was forced to sit at the back of the bus and drink from the "colored" drinking fountains. He had to use the "colored" restrooms and could only eat in certain restaurants.

How would you answer that question? I explained to him that the "Jim Crow" practices he experienced have been absent in America for several decades. I told him that most of the racist attitudes have also vanished, but that bigots still exist in all races. I spoke with him for over an hour, and he wanted to talk about only one thing: treatment of 'colored people' in America today. He asked about skin whitening cream, hiring practices, voting rights, home rental policies, and whether or not he could use any restroom or drinking fountain he chose.

His view of America, and consequently, Americans, was shaped by what he experienced more than half a century ago. I have no doubt that he shared his experiences with his children and grandchildren, and they may also have a distorted view of our culture based on family experience. What happens to family members, classmates, or neighbors when they travel abroad shapes opinion here. If someone they know was mistreated by a Saudi employer, it can shape the opinions of an entire community about the character of Saudi citizens. It's the same with Canadians, Australians, Americans, and Germans ... one bad character has the potential to impact how people feel about us before they even meet us.

A Brazilian visiting Baler made it known that he wanted to pay to have sex with young girls. He was boisterous and obnoxious. My wife overheard others talking about the "American," and tried to set the record straight – he was *Brazilian*. All foreigners here are automatically assumed to be Americans, so, by default, we bear the sins of all nationalities. As missionaries, we need to understand that we will face cultural bias. Most people on the planet have a preconceived opinion of Americans; it may be tainted by Hollywood, world politics, or a rowdy Brazilian, but we need to realize that we may be carrying baggage that we're unaware of.

So it's imperative as missionaries that we speak out of humility instead of superiority. Our way is not better, it's just different. There's a missionary here from Europe whom I've met who seems to hate all things Filipino. He complains about the food, the lack of organization, the laziness of the people, the corruption in government, wickedness in the church, the poor education system, and even the weather. He complains openly in front of Filipinos *about Filipinos*, who demonstrate their commitment to Christ by not punching him in the mouth. Avoid cultural judgment while on mission trips, and don't vocalize anything that you don't want overheard.

Our church in Georgia launched a campaign to purchase sacks of rice for poor families in the Philippines. Remarkably, more than one person purchased rice at the grocery store and handed a bag to me after Sunday worship services. Why would we buy rice in America, then ship it halfway around the world to a rice growing region? Rice is better and cheaper here in the Philippines! I must have communicated our intent quite poorly. Yet we do the same thing with other items, buying and shipping things like rubber flip flops that can be purchased for less in other nations. Not only is it cheaper to buy them here, it helps the local economy. They all come from China no matter where you source them. Unless there's a clear difference in the quality or price of an item, consider sourcing what you need in the nation you're visiting. It eliminates shipping charges and possible customs issues at the port.

Sometimes, we show our haughtiness by the things that we send to other nations. If you're shipping used clothing and shoes, please remove items that are soiled, torn, or worn beyond further use. If you wouldn't give it to your neighbor in need, don't ship it here! A man I admire bought every clothing item at a garage sale for only $5.00 and was surprised when I began sorting through the plastic garbage bags full of clothes, removing items that were no longer serviceable. He told me, "If they truly have nothing, they'll be grateful for these." It was a kind gesture to purchase the items, but he's not the one who will hand some poor woman a worn out, soiled dress to replace her other worn out torn dress. Save the rags to be used as rags – don't spend money to ship them to be given to people who are already wearing rags. Where's the love in that?

Local farmers here in Aurora plant vegetable crops that mature in sixty or ninety days. They want to get a return on their investment as quickly as possible. They wouldn't consider using their land to plant fruit orchards that require many years to produce a return. Too often we, as short term missionaries, take on the same attitude as our local farmers by looking for immediate results. Short term mission efforts seldom consider what they can do to produce fruit many years down the road. Some count the number of people who pray the sinner's

prayer. Others count the number of patients treated. It's much more

difficult to measure long term impact, so we use measurements that

can be reported to our church when we return home. "We had 570

salvations!" "We built three houses!" "We treated 612 patients!"

Examine your effort for long term impact.

Whether it's due to Hollywood, previous encounters with

Americans, or ancient history between cultures there are

preconceptions we must overcome when serving as missionaries.

Humility overpowers objections to our presence. Let's not do anything

to reinforce the stereotype of the 'ugly American.'

*Therefore, as God's chosen people, holy and dearly loved, clothe yourself
with compassion, kindness, humility, gentleness and patience. -
Colossians 3:12*

Chapter Twenty Eight Discussion Questions

1. How are people from your country viewed in the region where you are going?

2. Describe historical ties between your nation and the one you're visiting.

3. Is nationalism strong in the country you're visiting? How are foreigners treated?

4. Which items would be better to purchase in the country you're visiting?

5. Are there any items that would be better to purchase and ship ahead of time?

6. Has your team examined long-term benefit to your host ministry?

29 Re-entry

Short term missions can have a profound effect on people. Some missionaries arrive home and immediately clean out their closets, give away their surplus clothes and shoes, and urge others to do the same. Because of their close contact with people who have so little, God convicts them of their excess. They become acutely aware of their blessings and gain a heart of mercy for those who live in poverty.

Others react differently, becoming disillusioned with their own culture and they become vocally critical of the rampant materialism they see. They are awakened to the shallowness of American pop culture and view it with disgust. They experience reverse culture shock, becoming cynical and judgmental about their own culture. They may view their home church as apathetic when nobody seems interested to know more about their mission experience. And after experiencing passionate worship in another culture, they may view worship in their home church as lifeless, unenthusiastic, and completely devoid of passion. When you return home, please don't accuse your home church of apathy because they display their passion differently than what you experienced elsewhere.

Expect the following when you return:

- Friends will show only *limited* interest in your trip;

- People may want to see a *few* photos of your trip, but they're really not interested in the accompanying narrative or the whole album;

- Even family members don't want to watch *unedited* video of your trip;

- Any promises you made (raising funds, obtaining pledges etc.) will be difficult to fulfill.

Don't be surprised, or take it personally, when people aren't excited about your mission experience. Even ardent Christians in your church may seem dismissive and avoid talking about your trip. Mission work is tolerated, not celebrated, in many churches. Some may feel guilty about not going or helping to send others, and they feel awkward about discussing your trip. Others are genuinely unconcerned about missions, and could care less about your trip. Most, in my experience, want to know as much about it as they do your last vacation, "Well that's nice." They may, in fact, view it as more of a vacation than your response to the Lord's call. Expect lukewarm responses when you talk about your trip with other people – especially non-believers.

Some return home from mission trips and resume their normal routine, seemingly unaltered by their experience; yet for other team members the experience was transformational. It's all they think and talk about. There is no right or wrong way to feel when you return home, just don't expect others to relate to what you've been through. Some, perhaps, are honestly called to be missionaries, and even a taste of the mission field is exhilarating. Others may be called to become accountants. Some will become missionary accountants. I'm grateful for my calling as a missionary to the Philippines!

[16] But not all the Israelites accepted the good news. For Isaiah says, "Lord, who has believed our message?"[17] Consequently, faith comes from hearing the message, and the message is heard through the word about Christ. - Romans 10:16-17

Chapter Twenty Nine Discussion Questions

1. How can you minimize 'reverse culture shock'?

2. Are you prepared to accept disinterest from others regarding your mission trip?

3. Will you plan to select a small number of powerful photos to share and limit the entire album to only those who request to see more?

4. Who will edit your team video?

5. Has your team discussed 're-entry' issues?

30 You're home, not done

Mission complete! The long trip home is complete and you can sleep, once again, in your own bed. You can savor that bowl of Cinnamon Toast Crunch® and slowly spoon out every bite of your low fat blueberry yoghurt at breakfast. The 24-hour news channel droning in the background numbs your mind, as you sort through the large stack of unopened mail. Your yard is overgrown and needs attention, and your boss left five urgent voicemail messages on your answering service in the past three days. Your jungle mission experience is now a thing of the past and memories have been moving away at light speed, disappearing beyond our galaxy.

Your busy life resumes and consumes you. Your mission team didn't plan any follow-up meetings, and you weren't one of the three people selected to provide testimony to the church next Sunday. So you are officially *done* with your mission trip, right? I don't think so.

If you are asked to speak to the church, please tell them what was *accomplished* during the trip. You can tell your family and friends about the food that you refused to eat, how horribly you suffered from motion sickness as you travelled through the mountains, the movies you watched on the endless plane ride, or what you bought as souvenirs at the airport gift shop. But tell the church what it is hungry to hear. The church wants to know about souls won for Christ. Did your trip impact eternity? Tell them about it! Share anecdotes about the power of the Holy Spirit that was present while visiting a specific home. Or explain the impact that someone had on you during your visit. Don't share your mission trip with the church as if it was a vacation trip.

Unless you funded your entire trip without help, you have people that you need to thank; they invested in the mission and deserve to know how the Lord used you. If they live nearby, arrange a time to visit with them. Bring along a few photos that illustrate your role on the team. If your team creates an edited video, provide them with a copy. Let them know that you value their participation. If they live outside of your immediate area, call them and tell them how much you appreciate their help. Tell them about the highlight of your trip, and let them know how God was glorified. Make sure that they also receive a few good photos and any edited video of your trip. So now you're done, right? Nope.

If your team leader didn't schedule one, request a meeting with other team members to review the effectiveness of your trip. You met faithfully every week as you prepared for the trip, so what's one more meeting? When you get together, ask yourselves the following questions:

- What would you do differently knowing what you now know?

- What would you add to the list of items to bring along?

- Would you change any of the travel arrangements?

- Could we have been better prepared? How?

- Was our ministry effective?

- What could make our next trip more effective?

- How was God glorified by our effort?

- What was, personally, most demoralizing?

- Have we made any promises or commitments that need to be followed up?
- Are there things we can still do to maximize our effort as a team?

Most mission teams disintegrate once they arrive home. But there are normally loose ends that need to be tied up. Unless someone is a professional photographer and plans to sell their trip photos, make arrangements to collect everyone's digital photos and burn them to a DVD for everyone to share. Recruit someone to edit all of the team's video into a short presentation to show to the church. Make copies for team members to provide to all who made the trip possible. So after your debriefing meeting, photo swap, and video production are completed you are done, right? Not so fast.

Your host missionary would also like some feedback. As a team, take the time to assess your accommodations, in-country travel arrangements, food preparation, and overall organization. What could have made your trip better? What worked perfectly? Name anyone who was indispensible, or who went out of their way to assist you. Be honest in your assessment and help make future trips better. You're almost finished.

Ask your host missionary to provide your team leader with a confidential critique of your effort. This is not a 'thank you' letter that will be read to the church, it's a chance to know whether or not you hit or missed the mark. A truly honest assessment requires confidentiality because it may single out the behavior or lack of contribution of certain individuals. Any such critique should remain only with your church staff. Your best bet would be to provide a questionnaire to request what you would like to know. You'll discover that most missionaries have learned to 'speak the truth in love', so you'll likely get some positive feedback mixed with an expression of gratitude and a heartfelt invitation to return as soon as you are able.

So you're done now, right? Almost.

Please continue to pray for the ministry that you visited. Be specific. Include names. Ask the Lord to keep them united, to grow them in knowledge and faith, and to provide for their needs. And know that they will also be praying for you. *Now you're done.*

I have brought you glory on earth by completing the work you gave me to do. - John 17:4

Chapter Thirty Discussion Questions

1. Who from your team will share their testimony with the church during worship?

2. Are you willing to visit local supporters in person to thank them and share a copy of the team video or photos?

3. Will you call those who live outside of the immediate area to offer thanks?

4. Has your team scheduled a meeting after your return to assess your effectiveness?

5. Have you provided your host missionary with any constructive feedback?

6. Will you ask your host missionary to critique your team's contribution to the ministry?

7. Will you continue to pray for the needs of the ministry?

Attachment 1 - Mission Team Requirements

Eligibility Requirements

To become a team member, you must meet the following criteria:

- Be a born-again Christian who professes Jesus Christ as Lord and Savior;
- Believe that the Holy Bible is the inerrant Word of God;
- Be actively involved in one or more ministries of [our church];
- Non-church members need to provide a letter of reference from your pastor;
- Be 16 years of age or older (by departure date);
- Those under 18 years of age must be members of [our church] and complete application process with parental involvement;
- Personal interviews are required for each team member.

Individual Requirements

Failure to meet any of the following requirements will result in removal from the team.

- Each team member must read and sign the personal covenant and liability release form.
- Attendance at all team meetings is expected. A calendar of meetings and dates will be given at the first team meeting. Depending on the work-load, additional meetings may be added.
- Be ready and willing to share your testimony in front of the team or wherever the need may arise. On the field, you will need to be ready to share your testimony at a moment's notice!
- We will work through a Bible Study/Workbook as a team at each meeting. Assignments should be completed before each meeting so we can grow together and have discussions that will promote unity and growth within the team.
- There will be training and projects to get the team ready to go. Participation is mandatory. (For example, should we plan to do a puppet show while on the field, we may hold an event at our church which would give us a chance to "practice" as a team prior to the trip.)

- Background checks will be completed on each team member who has not already been background checked by [our church].
- While on the field, all team members will be asked to abide by the dress code established by the team leader.
- Meet all financial deadlines. Payments, deposits, and support raised are non-refundable.
- Willingly remove yourself from the team if something arises in your personal life that would cause you to be a stumbling block to the team.
- No drugs, alcohol, or tobacco are permitted on the mission trip.
- Submit to the authority of the team leader at all times as well as the Missionaries we'll be working with on the field.

Team Requirements

In signing on as a team member, you become part of a team and lose all individual privileges. All decisions and choices must be made as a team. The question of individual preferences must always be answered with, "How does it affect the entire group?" This is not an easy task. Consider the following:

- You must stay with the group. No wandering off alone.
- The team will eat all meals together unless a team member is sick (or other arrangements have been made)
- You must be on time for all functions.
- The Holy Spirit leads the team leader and the team must follow the leader at all times.
- The team follows the leadership of the missionary we are assigned to.

Attachment 2 - Sample Mission Trip Timeline and Deadlines

The following schedule is subject to change. Team members will be notified through the e-mail address you've provided regarding schedule changes.

August 2010

We will distribute information folders which provide a brief overview of the trip to Aurora including cost, dates, and details of the trip. We'll begin to form our team roster during this month.

September 2010

19   *Commitment Time!* Our first team meeting will be held at 7:30PM in choir room. We will collect deposits ($200), paperwork, (forms, application, liability waivers, covenant form, etc), and distribute Bible Study Workbooks.

20   Passport Applications must be submitted by this date to ensure enough time to process your application. (If possible, apply for your passport earlier than this date!)

26   Team Meeting (7:30PM). Discussion of Chapter 1 in Study Workbook. Bring your support letters (or a copy of your letter) to pray over as a team. Begin emphasis for testimonies, evangelism, and Tagalog skills.

30   Absolute last day to mail support letters.

October 2010

4   Plan to obtain immunizations now! Some, such as Hepatitis B require three doses a couple of weeks apart. (See the Immunization Form in your info packet for details on which shots you may need.)

10   Team Meeting (7:30PM). Discussion of Chapter 2 in Study Workbook. Personal Testimonies.

17   Team Meeting (7:30PM). Discussion of Chapter 3 in Study Workbook. Evangelism Study.

24   Team Meeting (7:30PM). Discussion of Chapter 4 in Study Workbook. Tagalog Skills.

November 2010

7   Team Meeting (7:30PM). Discussion of Chapters 5 & 6 in Study Workbook.

14   Team Meeting (7:30PM). Overview and Summary of Study Workbook, continued spiritual preparation. Team preparations (evangelism review, Tagalog skills, testimonies, balloons, etc). Evaluate account balances, pray for support that is still needed.

29   Deadline for airline ticket money. You are responsible to provide the funds to purchase your ticket if your support is not sufficient at this time. *(Note: We will not meet on this day, but support must be turned in to church office by 5PM.)*

December 2010

6   Our one and only meeting in December. Plan to be there before we break for the holidays! It will take place in the fellowship hall at 7PM. *(Note: This meeting is on a Monday night.)*

January 2010

2   Team Meeting at 5:00PM in choir room (time subject to change). Prepare bins, assign travel partners, tie up loose ends, and review our mission. Only one meeting left as of this date!

9   Commissioning Service for the team in both Morning Worship Services at [our church.] Plan to be present for both services.

9   Final Team Meeting at 7:30PM (time subject to change). This meeting will finalize our plans to get to the airport, assign any remaining baggage, and make sure all final preparations are complete. Pray, prepare, finish packing!

15   Depart for Maria Aurora, Philippines

28   Return home

February 2011

7   Team Report in both morning worship services at [our church.]

Attachment 3 - Passport Procedures

To travel overseas, all team members will be required to have their own US Passport. See below for some guidelines and tips if you do not have a passport.

1. Those who already have a passport should check to make sure it will be valid while on the trip. (Some countries require that your passport be valid for at least 90 days even though you are traveling for only two weeks.)

2. For detailed information, go to www.travel.state.gov/passport for information related to applying for a passport, renewing a passport, or replacing a lost or stolen passport.

3. Contact a local Post Office for information and/or the application itself (not all Post Offices can provide this service).

   - The Post Office on Main Street will most-likely be the best place to handle the process.
   - Be sure to call ahead as most Post Offices have special hours for receiving passport applications.

4. It will take at least 6-8 weeks to receive your passport, so it is vital you begin the process immediately!

5. See a fellow team member or your team leader if you have any questions or need further guidance.

Barry D. Phillips

Attachment 4 - Sample Covenant & Liability Release Form

[Our Church]

The guidelines listed below are recommended for those participating in our trip the Philippines. You are not traveling as a tourist, but as a guest of another country, and as an ambassador for Jesus Christ. The Philippines is considered an underdeveloped nation and does not have the conveniences that you are used to at home. It is important for you to be flexible, patient, and willing to adjust to the expectations of your host.

I recognize and accept the following conditions which will further the usefulness and safety of our short-term mission. If accepted as a member of this team, I agree to:

1. Release and discharge [our church], which helped make these arrangements, their agents, employees, officers, and volunteers from all claims, demands, actions, judgments, or executions that I have ever had, or now have, or may have, or which my heir, executors, administrators, or assigns may have or claim to have, against their organization, their agents, their employees, officers, and volunteers and their successors or assigns, for all personal injuries, known or unknown, and injuries to property, real or personal, caused by, or arising out of this journey. I intend to be legally bound by this statement.
2. Adopt an attitude that I am on this team to try to understand host culture, not to convince them of my own viewpoint or style. I go with an understanding that there are many different ways to accomplish the same objective, and know that my way is not necessarily the best.
3. Abstain from making derogatory comments or arguments regarding people, politics, sports, religion, race, or traditions.
4. Go as a servant-disciple of Jesus Christ and I will adopt that attitude when dealing with my fellow team members and the people I meet during the trip.
5. Accept and submit to the leadership role and authority of the team leader and promise to abide by his or her decisions as they concern this mission trip.
6. Acknowledge that by engaging in this journey, I am subjecting myself to

228

certain risks voluntarily, including and in addition to those risks that I normally face in my personal and business life, including, but not limited to: health hazards due to poor food and water, diseases, pests, poor sanitation, potential danger from lack of control over local population, potential injury while working, and inadequate medical facilities.

7. Understand that our team's work is but a tiny speck on the bigger picture that our mission partners are trying to accomplish. I promise not to be overly demanding, to do my best not to offend or cause embarrassment for the local mission host, and to do my best to help them accomplish their long term goals.

8. Attend all team meetings, both prior to departure and during the mission trip.

9. Expeditiously follow up on all requirements for passports, visas, financial obligations, vaccinations, travel insurance, etc.

10. Refrain from meddling, complaining, and obscene or insensitive humor. I realize that others on my team during the journey and while onsite view me as an example of how a Christian acts, and I will not treat that responsibility lightly. I understand that travel, especially to remote locations, can be difficult, and I promise to adopt a flexible attitude and be supportive as plans may need to be changed. I understand that I must travel with the rest of the team (team members will not be permitted to arrive early or extend their stay on the mission field).

11. Regard the differing styles of worshipping with respect. I promise that where I see the need, I will witness my faith, but without a superior, colonial attitude.

12. If a loved one or dear friend is traveling with me, we agree to interact with all members of the team, not just one another. I promise not to initiate or seek new romantic relationships with team members or the nationals during the trip.

13. Avoid any actions which might be perceived as amorous toward indigenous people I meet.

14. Refrain from using tobacco or alcoholic beverages while in the host country. Abstain from using any illegal drugs or prohibited activity while on this trip.

15. Remember that we will be watched very closely. I will not take lightly this important responsibility of setting an example.

16. Refrain from giving gifts such as: money, clothes, jewelry, tape players, etc. Although the intent of the giver is good, the result after we leave

has caused problems for our host, and jealously and bitterness amongst those locals who received no such largesse. If I feel compelled to give a gift to someone I've met, I will consult first with the team leader before I promise or give the gift, and I promise to let him or her make the final decision on this matter. This covenant does not apply to the small fellowship tokens we will discuss and have approved before leaving home.

17. Act as a servant-disciple of the local pastor or mission organization. I will respect the advice I am given concerning attire, eating, drinking, and other traditions that may help me assimilate into the local community.

18. Understand that every member of this group is expected to share freely from their particular blessings and talents, whether that is skills such as music, art, carpentry, or basic hard work. I agree to participate in these ways as fully as possible.

19. I agree that in the event my conduct during the trip is considered so unsatisfactory that it jeopardizes the success of the trip, and that medication during the trip has failed to correct my behavior that my services in connection with this mission shall end and I shall return home immediately at my own expense.

20. In signing below, I represent that I am 18 years of age or older, or my parent/guardian will sign also, accepting the above conditions on my behalf.

Team member's printed name and signature

Legal guardian's printed name and signature

Attachment 5 - Sample Support Letter

Uncle Bubba,   5/7/10

[Our Church] is sponsoring a mission trip to the Philippines in July and I feel that God is leading me to participate. Our team will leave Savannah on January 17 and will remain in the remote Aurora Province northeast of Manila for two weeks. A variety of ministry activities are planned. We will be painting Malupa Baptist Church, distributing donated items (such as pre-packed Christmas Shoeboxes), visiting schools with craft activities to share the Gospel, and we have planned puppet shows, movies, and other activities to share Jesus with the children of the area as well. I'm excited about what the Lord has planned during this trip.

[Our Church] has taken eight previous mission trips to the Aurora Province and the results have been amazing. We delivered clothing, toiletries, toys, and other donated items to hundreds of households, using the opportunity to share the Gospel of Christ. Our teams have taught women to sew and donated several sewing machines to help them generate an income for their families. Several men constructed a public restroom for a local church. Crafts, music, and puppet shows allowed children to have great fun as they also heard the message of Jesus. As a result, well over one thousand people have come to know Jesus as Lord and Savior! Our team returned from the most recent trip with contagious enthusiasm and unity in spirit, and I feel led to participate in the coming trip in January.

Each member of our mission team has been asked to build a support team to provide prayer, encouragement, and financial assistance. I've included you as a member of my support team. Please pray that our team will remain safe and healthy for the duration of this trip. Pray that God will open the hearts of those that we'll encounter, and use us to demonstrate Christ's love. If you are able to provide financial assistance, please follow the instructions on the enclosed slip and send any contribution directly to our church. The total cost for our mission trip is about $2,000. This includes round trip airfare from Savannah to Manila, lodging, food, and ground transportation to and from the Aurora Province - not bad for a two week trip halfway around the world, but I need help in raising funds. Please note that the deadline for contributions has been established by our team leader as December 8; I'll pay the balance of all expenses not received by this date.

Thanks for your prayers and support. You've always been a blessing to me,

In His Service,

[Missionary Name]

Attachment 6 - Sample Support Raising Policy

Financial Support Guidelines:

To be involved in missions, whether at the stateside or international level, is a challenge which reaps great rewards for all involved. One of the greatest rewards happens to involve what is often the most challenging step: raising financial support. It has been the experience of many that the raising of financial support has proven to be one of the most rewarding parts of the entire mission's process. Through the support-raising process, faith is challenged, prayer support is received, a personal mission "team" is formed for the individual, and God is glorified as the Provider which He promises to be. Yes, raising financial support is a rewarding experience! With this in mind, please note below some of the specific guidelines which [Our Church] implements to help make this process most effective.

Support letters must be mailed no later than the deadline set by your Team Leader. We will require team members to bring the finished letters (or a copy of your letter) to a team meeting so that we can pray over them. We will also keep a copy of your letter on file with your important documents. Also included in the letter must be a **Support Response Form** (enclosed in folder) to give specific instructions to the contributor concerning their contribution (see enclosed sample support letter).

Contributions by others on your behalf are to be made by check to [Our Church]. All contributions are to be mailed to or given to [Our Church] 123 Main Street, Anytown, USA, 11111

A specific dollar amount to be contributed to you by [Our Church] will be determined **after** an initial team roster is established. This contribution will be a maximum amount to be applied in the event that all of your support is not raised. This amount *will only be applied after airline tickets have been purchased*. This figure will differ from trip to trip and will be drawn from the [Our Church] Global Missions account and is available for church members only.

The amount needed for the purchase of your airline ticket is **due in full** before your ticket will be purchased. On the date set for airline funds to be due, if your support is not sufficient to satisfy that amount, the remainder will be required from you personally or else no ticket will be purchased for you. In the event that you must pay "out of pocket", you will be reimbursed to the amount that support comes in on your behalf up to thirty days after the trip concludes. This reimbursement will **not** include your initial non-refundable trip deposit.

In the event that support is raised by an individual above the required trip amount, all overage will be applied equally to the remaining members of the team. This will apply also in the event that support is raised by a team member who is later unable to participate in the mission trip.

Thank you for your consideration in participating in the upcoming [Our Church] mission trip! As God leads you in this step of faith, know that He will be faithful to provide for every need along the way.

Support Letter Process/Guidelines:

- Prepare the supporter (contributor) list (a minimum of 25 people; friends, family, Christian contacts, others).
- Write your own letter (see sample letter enclosed for ideas). The last thing a donor wants is four copies of the same letter with four different signatures. People prefer to read a personal letter—so add your personal touch!
- Send the letter, support response form, and a self addressed/stamped envelope to the list of potential supporters. Be sure these are mailed out by the deadline set by the team leader to allow time for your support to be received.
- You will be notified of all support which comes in on your behalf, and regular updates on the status of your account will be provided by team leader at the meetings.
- Write thank you notes to your supporters within a week of receiving support.
- Send a follow-up letter within three weeks of your return to describe what happened on the trip and how it changed your life (include pictures, etc).

Attachment 7- Sample Team Member Checklist

The following is a list of items that must be completed for the trip. Failure to take care of business on schedule causes delays for the entire team and additional expenses we cannot afford to incur while being good stewards of the financial support that is raised for the team. You will not be considered a team member until all items below have been completed, so check carefully!

☐   Application turned in

☐   Personal testimony completed (turned in with application)

☐   Personal Covenant and Liability Release Form turned in

☐   Passport copies turned in (two copies to church, one copy to keep at home)

☐   Copy of Support Letter turned in

☐   Support letters completed (typed, stuffed, mailed, etc)

☐   Minor Escort Form turned in (for those under 18; be sure it is notarized)

☐   Background Check Form turned in

☐   Non-refundable deposit turned in

☐   Letter or Recommendation from pastor turned in (for non-church members)

Attachment 8 – Sample Mission Application

[Our Church]

PERSONAL INFORMATION (Please Print Clearly)

Full name: _____ Date: _____

Current address:

_____

City: _____ State: _____ Zip: _____

Home phone: _____ Cell phone: _____

Work phone: _____

Email address: _____

Date of birth: _____ Age: _____

Social Security Number: _____

Citizenship: _____ Country of birth: _____

Marital status: _____ If married, list spouse name: _____

If Applicable, List Names and Ages of Children:

_____

Occupation: _____

EMERGENCY CONTACT INFORMATION

Name: _____

Relationship to you: _____

Home phone: _____ Cell phone: _____

Work phone:_____

Name: _____

Relationship to you: _____

Home phone: _____ Cell phone: _____

Work phone: _____

If Under the Age of 18, Please List Parent(s) Name(s):

_____

Have You Talked to Your Parents About Short Term Missions? ☐
Yes ☐ No

Are They Supportive? ☐ Yes ☐ No

If No, Please Explain:

_____

_____

PASSPORT INFORMATION

Do you have a passport? ☐ Yes ☐ No ☐ In progress

Name on passport: _____

Passport number: _____

Date of Issue: _____

Date of expiration: _____

City and State of issue: _____

REFERENCE INFORMATION

Please provide two references. One reference should be from an individual outside of [Our Church]. Both references should be from people who know your ministry abilities/experiences as well as your strengths and weaknesses.

Reference #1 - Name: _____

Relationship to You: _____

Phone Number: _____

Email Address: _____

Reference #2 - Name: _____

Relationship to You: _____

Phone Number: _____

Email Address: _____

MEDICAL INFORMATION

Do you have any physical condition that may limit your ability to perform ministry activities (based on the conditions which are outlined in your info packet)? ☐ Yes ☐ No

If yes, please describe:

_____

Are you currently taking <u>any</u> medications? ☐ Yes ☐ No

If yes, please list all medications (including non-prescriptions):

Are you currently under a doctor's care or have you been in the last year?

 ☐ Yes ☐ No

If yes, please explain:

Have you had any major surgery or major health problems within the past two years? ☐ Yes ☐ No   If yes, please explain:

Do you have any special dietary needs? ☐ Yes ☐ No   If yes, please explain:

Do you have any known allergies? ☐ Yes ☐ No   If yes, please explain:

CHURCH INVOLVEMENT/MINISTRY EXPERIENCE

Church membership: ☐ [Our Church]   ☐ Other church:

If not a member of a church, do you attend a church regularly? ☐ Yes ☐ No   If yes, where?

List the ministries with which you have been involved at your church. Include time of involvement and any leadership positions held:

List the ministries with which you have been involved outside of your church. Include time of involvement and any leadership positions held:

Please describe your strengths:

Please describe your weaknesses or areas in which you desire growth:

_____

_____

How would you describe your daily relationship with Jesus Christ?

_____

_____

FIELD OF INTEREST

Is this your first foreign mission trip? ☐ Yes ☐ No

If no, list previous mission trip locations:

_____

How do you know God has called you to participate in this trip?

_____

_____

Please indicate any special talents that you feel may be helpful while on the field (foreign language training, skills, Christian service experience, etc):

Do you have any training in evangelism? If so, explain:

_____

Please share your salvation testimony. Include how long you've been a believer and how you were saved (Please attach a separate piece of paper.)

PARTICIPATION AGREEMENT

I acknowledge that the information provided on this application is complete and accurate to the best of my knowledge. I have read, understand, and will abide by all the guidelines, requirements, and policies outlined in the information folder. I realize that failure to do so could result in my removal from the team.

_____

Team Member's Signature   Date

_____

Parent Signature (if team member is under 18)   Date

Attachment 9 - Sample Consent for Minor Form

Travel Consent for Minor on Mission Trip to the Philippines
(Please PRINT using black ink.)

Minor Child Information

Passport name: _____

Address: _____

Gender: _____ Date of birth: _____

Country of birth: _____ Nationality: _____

Passport number: _____ Passport issue date: _____

Passport issue location: _____

Telephone number: _____

Parent name: _____

Address: _____

Home phone number: _____

Work phone number: _____

Cell phone number: _____

Email address: _____

Parent/Guardian Information

Planned Travel Dates: Departure _____ Return _____

Origin of trip: _____

Destination: _____

I authorize the above named escort, whose signature is affixed below mine, to accompany my minor child and act in my behalf during the entire travel period listed above.

Parent Signature: _____   Date: _____

Escort Signature: _____   Date: _____

Notary Signature: _____   Date: _____

Details and Signatures

Escort Name: _____

Address: _____

Passport Number: _____

Passport Issue Date: _____ Issue Location: _____

Relationship to Guardian: _____

Authorized to make medical decisions: YES   NO   (circle one)

END NOTES

i Christian Chronicle – "Are Short Term Missions Worth What they Cost?" Tryggestad, Erik, 1 Mar, 2006

ii Missionary Care, Resources for Missions and Mental Health, "Missionary Marriage Issues, This is No Honeymoon", Dr. Kotesky, Ronald, 2008

iii Neumann, Craig S.; Hare, Robert D. (2008). "Psychopathic traits in a large community sample: Links to violence, alcohol use, and intelligence.". *Journal of Consulting and Clinical Psychology* **76** (5): 893.doi:10.1037/0022-006X.76.5.893.PMID 18837606. [http://www.safe-nz.org.nz/Articles/conscience.htm

iv Harris, Grant; Rice, Marnie (2006). "Treatment of psychopathy: A review of empirical findings". In Patrick, Christopher. *Handbook of Psychopathy*. pp. 555–572.

www.ingramcontent.com/pod-product-compliance
Lightning Source LLC
Chambersburg PA
CBHW060011050426

42448CB00012B/2704